The Human Side of Christ

Meet the Guy Behind the God

Will Hathaway

www.will-hathaway.com

Creative Team Publishing
San Diego

© 2013 by Will Hathaway.

All rights reserved. No part of this book may be reproduced, stored in a retrieval system or transmitted in any form or by any means without the prior written permission of the publisher, except by a reviewer who may quote brief passages in a review to be distributed through electronic media, or printed in a newspaper, magazine or journal.

Permissions and Credits:

Scripture quotations taken from the New American Standard Bible®, Copyright © 1960, 1962, 1963, 1968, 1971, 1972, 1973, 1975, 1977, 1995 by The Lockman Foundation Used by permission." (www.Lockman.org)

Blue Letter Bible. "Dictionary and Word Search for *harpagmos (Strong's 725)*". Blue Letter Bible. 1996-2013. 9 Feb 2013.
< http:// www.blueletterbible.org/lang/lexicon/lexicon.cfm?Strongs=G725&t=KJV >

Blue Letter Bible. "Dictionary and Word Search for *kenoō (Strong's 2758)*". Blue Letter Bible. 1996-2013. 9 Feb 2013.
< http:// www.blueletterbible.org/lang/lexicon/lexicon.cfm?Strongs=G2758&t=NASB >

A variety of stories are presented in the book to illustrate concepts and points about God's interaction with mankind. All the stories are true. Some of these are direct accounts for which permission was obtained for their use. Others, for which permission was not obtained, employ fictitious characters and events in order to protect the identities of those involved. Any resemblance to actual names of people, situations, companies or events is purely coincidental.

ISBN: 978-0-9884934-2-1
PUBLISHED BY CREATIVE TEAM PUBLISHING
www.CreativeTeamPublishing.com
San Diego
Printed in the United States of America

Endorsements on Behalf of

The Human Side of Christ

Victoria Lee
Oklahoma Author
Host of "Making It Happen TV"

In reading Will Hathaway's book I found myself weaved through many of the pages. Often the questions he posed were thoughts I had pondered. I've needlessly found myself confused by the religious bondages that restrained me from living a life full of freedom.

Will's perspective in *The Human Side of Christ* leaves us feeling less obligated to be so "perfect" and more willing to give ourselves permission to "just be." In allowing God to transform us by His love rather than a set of rules, we become more like the image of Christ we are seeking to be.

Thank you Will for your insight—your willingness to raise questions and of course those occasional bits of humor.

*****

Dave Curtiss
Vice President of Faith Engagement
CHRISTA Ministries
www.crista.org

I truly enjoyed the open and honest portrayal of the real person of Jesus the Christ in "The Human Side of Christ." As a young Christian I often wrestled with the "over-deification" of Jesus and was left feeling that Christian holiness was absolutely unattainable in my imperfect life.

In his excellent book, Will Hathaway reveals the real Jesus, the perfect union of immanent and transcendent, living a true-to-life reality in His Father's world. Will captures the candid and authentic life of Jesus who relates so well to each of us and the truth of our lives, and points us directly to the greatest hope of all, our Lord and Savior, the hope of the world, Jesus Christ.

*****

Heather Bixler
Author/Writer
www.HeatherBixler.com

Every time I read a book by Will Hathaway I find myself walking away with a new perspective on God, and a profound understanding of God's love, will, and desire for my life. *The Human Side of Christ* is no different. I truly love how Will has taken the life of Jesus and uses it to teach us how to live this very human life, and how to approach those difficult moments and questions. I will definitely be thinking on everything I have read in The Human Side of Christ for quite some time.

The Human Side of Christ

Meet the Guy Behind the God

Will Hathaway

Table of Contents

	Dedication	11
	Ordinary	13
1	Be a Man	23
2	Self-Discovery	31
3	Adorable	41
4	Salvation	57
5	Life to the Full	65
6	Denial or Self-Denial?	75
7	The Broken Law	83
8	Jesus and Sexuality	91
9	God's Plan	107
10	Jesus, the Recluse	117

11	The Rock Star	123
12	The Unanswered Prayer	131
13	The Faith to Believe	141

Extra-Ordinary	149
Acknowledgements	155
The Author	159
Speaking Engagements and Products	163

Dedication

I dedicate this book to You, a Jewish peasant, who lived 2,000 years ago. The debate about who and what you were still rages on today, all these years after your life. To some you are a legend, to others you are an ancient sage, many say you were a cult leader, and to me I am now more certain than ever that you are the very Son of God.

Regardless of how humanity labels you, I want to thank you. Thank you for showing us how to live, thank you for showing us how to extract the absolute most from our existence and, most of all, thank you for teaching us how to love. It was in studying you as my peer that I found you were most certainly not. I have now found an appreciation for you and the life you lived that is so much deeper than ever before.

Next I dedicate this book to my children. Thank you for showing me how to re-appreciate life by demonstrating the wonders of this world though your innocent little eyes. You all have given me a firsthand look at what it means to "come like a child."

Lastly, I dedicate this book to my wife, Karra. Thank you for sacrificing so many countless hours reading over my manuscripts and putting up with me constantly asking, "What if?" I love you.

Ordinary

I'm a guy. A pretty typical guy really, average size, average income, average life… balding. You get the idea. Don't get me wrong, though. I thoroughly enjoy my life… it's just average, and I like that. I have a hard time imagining what it would be like to have "rock star" status. I figure this is most likely because I've never experienced it. I couldn't relate to someone who has to make special arrangements just to go out to dinner so they don't get mobbed by adoring fans. I don't know what it's like to have millions of dollars in discretionary income.

I find it interesting when I observe a mega star who was just an average sort at one point: someone who is self-made, especially when it happens a little later in life. When I hear them talk or watch them interact, sometimes you can see they still remember what it's like just to be average and as a result, they don't take themselves too seriously. I tend to be more attracted to this type of individual because even though I don't know what it is like to live their life, they still have the ability to remember when they had an average life similar to mine.

Morgan Freeman is one of my favorite actors. I've never met him but in the few interviews I've seen with him, he seems like such a down to earth guy. He doesn't seem to act and talk like a "celebrity" to me. Then I happened to come across a show doing a biography on him and discovered he didn't get his big break until he was in his 50's! Prior to that, he was mostly a starving actor just trying to make ends meet. He knows what it's like to be an average Joe because for most of his life he was one. And, based on the biography interviews I saw, he clearly hasn't forgotten what it was like to be a regular guy.

On the other hand, when someone attains their great fame either at a very early age or was born to famous parents, they often seem to have little concept of what it is like to possess an average normal life.

Personally, I have a more difficult time with this type of celebrity because I really have no idea what it is like to be them, and they have no idea of what it is like to be me. There is so much less to connect with.

During my life, I've kind of felt the same way about God. I really don't know what it is like to be God. It seems like it would be pretty cool, but I really don't know. It's difficult for me to grasp the idea of being an all powerful, omnipresent, and immortal creature, living outside of time. Well, actually let me think about it a little more… nope, I just can't quite make the connection.

I have heard, though, that God once became a man, and as a result He can relate to me. Really? I have a little bit of a hard time with this one as well. Can a "God-Man" honestly have a good grasp of what it is like to be an average, ordinary human being? After all, I hear about Jesus reading people's minds, walking on water, and healing the sick. Can a guy who can do all that really have an idea of what it's like to be human? The Bible says that Jesus never even sinned! Not even once! Can a guy that has never sinned possibly know what it's like to be me?

One time when I was in college I had the opportunity to watch an ordination board at the church I was attending. An ordination board is normally the final step in the process of becoming an ordained minister. It is an opportunity for a bunch of pastors to ask a person, or a few persons in this case, a bunch of questions about the Bible to see how they answer them. If he or she answers them appropriately, then they will be approved for ordination.

This particular ordination board was open to the whole church to attend. So if these candidates weren't terrified enough by having to sit in front of a bunch of pastors dying to ask the most difficult questions they could possibly think of, they also had to do it while sitting on a stage in front of the whole congregation to see them sink or swim. It was kinda like an early version of reality TV.

I recall there being a number of difficult questions about the Bible these guys took turns answering brilliantly, all of which I have since forgotten; but then came the one I remembered. One of the pastors asked a question about the temptations of Christ. You see, before Jesus started His ministry, the Bible speaks of Him being led out into the wilderness where the devil tempted Him. Jesus spent 40 days fasting in the wilderness, and at the end it says He was hungry, which I'm guessing is a bit of an understatement. The devil then challenges Jesus to turn rocks into bread so He can eat, but Jesus refuses. The devil tempts Jesus two more times while He is in this weakened state, but Jesus stays true to the course and resists Satan.

When faced with this question, one of the young ordination candidates answered up that the temptation of Christ was not to show that He *would not* sin, but rather that Christ *could not* sin. It was a concept I had never really thought about before and, to be honest, I was impressed by his answer. I was in awe of the idea that Christ was so perfect He couldn't even sin!

That answer stuck with me, and one night several years later I suddenly ran into a bit of a road block. I was reading in the book of Hebrews and came across this passage: "For we do not have a high priest who cannot sympathize with our weaknesses, but One who has been tempted in all things as we are, yet without sin." (Hebrews 4:15)

It said that Christ was sympathetic to my plight as a man and my struggles with sin. In fact, He had been tempted in every way I had been tempted, yet without sin. All of a sudden it occurred to me, "So what if Christ never sinned!" He couldn't sin! And if He couldn't sin, what is so impressive about not sinning? That's like saying it's really impressive that a blind guy never looked lustfully at a woman. (Although if I was blind, I'd probably find a way to do it... I mean back when I was single, of course... now I only have eyes for my lovely wife.)

Then another thought occurred to me. If Christ couldn't sin, how could He really have been tempted? And if He was never tempted, then how could He possibly be able to relate to us? If Christ couldn't sin, then He had no idea what it was like to be one of us. This disappointed me because I really wanted to believe in a God who truly understood just how difficult it is to go through this life in the face of constant temptation, fear, and self-doubt. That is when I first decided to step out and consider an idea that, at the time, seemed like heresy: What if Christ could have sinned?

This was a rather uncomfortable concept, mainly because I feared going to Hell just for thinking it. It seemed much safer to think of a Christ that could not sin because that just seemed to be more holy. To think of a Christ who could sin felt like I was weakening Him in my mind, making Him too much like me. But then I found Philippians, Chapter 2: "Do nothing from selfishness or empty conceit, but with humility of mind regard one another as more important than yourselves; do not merely look out for your own personal interests, but also for the interests of others. Have this attitude in yourselves which was also in Christ Jesus, who, although He existed in the form of God, did not regard equality with God a thing to be grasped, but emptied Himself, taking the form of a bond-servant, and being made in the likeness of men. Being found in appearance as a man, He humbled Himself by becoming obedient to the point of death, even death on a cross." (Philippians 2:3-8)

I find this to be one of the most interesting little passages in the entire Bible. And it becomes even more intriguing the further we break it down. It says Christ existed in the "form of God" but "did not regard equality with God a thing to be grasped..." The direct translation of the word "grasped" is "harpagmos" which means "the act of seizing, robbery" (Strongs G725) and the direct translation of the word "emptied" is "kenoō" which means: "1) to empty, make empty; a) of Christ, he laid aside equality with or the form of God" (Strongs G2758)

So wait a second. What exactly does that mean? Of what, exactly, did He empty Himself? If I'm interpreting this correctly, it appears that as a human being, equality with God is not something that we are capable of possessing. No matter how hard we try, we cannot "rob" or "steal" the position that belongs to God. So, in order for Jesus to become a man, He had to "empty" Himself. He had to temporarily set aside His power and position as God in order to truly become a human!

Think about it, the book of Genesis says that we were made in the "image" of God. If being human is not to be God but to be in the image of God, then Jesus would have had to lower Himself to become a man. If He had not, He would not have been a man. If He emptied Himself of being God, then it means Jesus really was human! Just like you and me! Yeah, He was still God in *who* He was but He emptied Himself of being God in *what* He was.

Or let's look at it this way. Imagine a police officer who has jurisdiction in one state traveling to a state to where he has no jurisdiction. The guy is still a police officer in who he is as a person, but once he enters that other state, he has no access to his power as a police officer due to the fact that he is out of his jurisdiction. He is now a regular civilian just like everybody else. You could walk up to him and ask him *who* he was and he could honestly and truthfully say he was a police officer. But if you were to ask him *what* he was, in this instance he would have to say he was a civilian. It's almost like God took all of His Godness and set it aside to become a human, giving Himself no more access to His power than any of us would have.

If that's the case, if that really happened, then it means even though Jesus was God, He was still just like you and me. I have come to believe that Jesus could have sinned if He had wanted to. The difference is I don't think He ever wanted to. But could He have? Certainly! He had two arms and two legs, He had the ability to slap, punch, or hurt someone. He had a mouth and a tongue He could have used to slander, curse, or belittle. He had all the same capabilities to sin that we have. Yet, He was still without sin! Had Jesus not possessed the capability to sin, then His feat of sinlessness is not very impressive. But, if Jesus emptied Himself of what made Him God, leaving Him just as vulnerable to sin as we are and He still never sinned? How impressive is that?! In fact, in my mind, for Him to have lived a sinless life for 33 years on this earth with no more access to God than what any of the rest of us have was perhaps the most impressive of all of His miracles or feats. Save maybe the resurrection... maybe. I have to admit, given the option of a regular guy living a sinless life or someone being raised from the dead, I'm still not sure which would impress me more.

So if this was the case, if Jesus really was just like us, what else do we share in common with this amazing human being?

1

Be a Man

"Be a man!" my father barked out. It was dusty and cold as we were riding along on horseback following a herd of cattle. My behind was sore and my hand had developed a small blister from clutching the saddle horn. At the age of five, this was the second time I had ever "helped" with our annual roundup.

Each year in the fall after a week of gathering cattle from all corners of the ranch, a small army of cowboys would assemble in our kitchen for a pre-dawn breakfast. Then my brother, sister, and I would take our flashlights out in the early morning darkness to bridle and saddle the horses. As morning twilight began to break we would ride to the pasture where the cattle had been gathered and spend the next few hours herding them to the corrals to be separated for the large trucks that would later haul them off for sale. The horses were always restless and skittish this time of day. The temperatures were below freezing and blasts of vapor would shoot from their nostrils like dragons blowing smoke. I remember it was always hard to keep my hands warm on these frozen mornings, so as we rode I would reach back and take turns slipping them under the saddle blanket to warm them against the horse's body.

At such a young age, I really wasn't any help, but I enjoyed feeling like a real cowboy, wearing my cowboy hat, chaps, and riding our ancient steed named Lincoln. At almost 25 years old, he wasn't much help either but made the perfect nag for a five- year-old to clop along behind a cattle drive. About mid-morning I would start getting tired and begin to voice my desire to be done with our work for the day by asking how much longer. Eventually, my father would grow tired of my whining as my attention turned from the task at hand. It was at this point he would bark, "Be a man!" We then knew we had reached his complaint threshold and that it would be wise to be quiet for a while (he even directed the command to my sisters!). We always got a kick out of his demand for us and would often mockingly repeat it to each other. "Yeah, be a man!"

As a child I always felt like a man as long as I was on my horse. But I remember vividly getting quite nervous whenever I had to dismount my loyal friend in the middle of a corral filled with cattle. Atop the horse, I felt brave and fearless, but once down on my feet, the animals seemed huge. Most of them looked down on me and I would always stay close by the nearest adult trying to pretend that I wasn't the least bit afraid; then I would scamper through the fence as quickly as I could. The men always seemed so calm around the animals, never scared or intimidated. In my mind, I knew the cattle were, for the most part, tame and scared of us, but I was still timid. I would watch these guys as they tirelessly worked the herd. With calloused hands and the chime of spurs they would make their way around the corrals, working together as a team to accomplish the job. During the occasional break they would gather around the fire with a cup of coffee and whatever pastry the wives had brought, laughing and telling jokes in Spanish. I remember being so eager to grow up and be like them: to be tough, strong, and fearless, to be able to tame the wildest of broncos with skill and ease. Yes, as a boy I couldn't wait to grow up and fulfill my dad's request, I wanted to be like these guys, a true and real man.

Defining manliness has really been an elusive target in American history. When I was young I remember manliness being captured by guys like John Wayne, The Lone Ranger, or G.I. Joe. My wife would even say Charles Ingalls from *Little House on the Prairie*. Lately, manliness has been redefined by guys wearing skinny jeans, or by pasty vampires who look like they could blow away in the wind. Pretty boys to Cowboys, the definition of a man is certainly something that is in the eye of the beholder.

I recently conducted an unofficial poll asking female friends to describe "manliness" in a word and the responses included: provider, muscles, protector, physical and mental strength, spiritual, humble, leader, faith, maturity, stability, presence, servant, godly, strong, honor and dependable. So when we think of the idea of God becoming a man, what kind of a man would He have become? What exactly would God as a "man" look like? It's hard to say really, but one thing I do know is that from all the pictures, He clearly had some great hair.

We know a little bit about who Jesus was based on the Gospels, but honestly they aren't exactly a biography of the man. When we really get down to it, we know the guy was born, we know that when He was twelve He was conducting Bible studies that were profound even to the Professors of the Scriptures. We know when He was about 30, He engaged in a 3-year ministry that concluded with Him getting killed, resurrecting, and ascending into heaven. So, in all, out of a 33-year life, we have a few pages about a three-year ministry, one story about His childhood, the story of His birth, and the rest is shrouded in mystery.

When we consider God becoming a man, what we're really exploring is the personality of God. After all, if He "emptied" Himself of everything else that made Him God, one of the only things that would be left would be the personality. What would that look like? I suppose, because God is holy and good, this would result in a person who didn't lose His temper, drink, cheat, steal, smoke, dance, go to "R" rated movies, and always hung out with the good kids. But when we look at Jesus, we see He did do things like drink; I mean His first miracle helped a bunch of people get sloshed at a wedding! And the story doesn't really lend itself to any other conclusion: "When the headwaiter tasted the water which had become wine, and did not know where it came from (but the servants who had drawn the water knew), the headwaiter called the bridegroom, and said to him, 'Every man serves the good wine first, and when the people have drunk freely, then he serves the poorer wine; but you have kept the good wine until now.'" (John 2:9, 10)

According to this account, it sounds like people were already pretty lit prior to Jesus performing His party-enhancing feat. I'll be honest; I'll bet from then on all of His friends were like, "If this dude can turn water into wine, I'm having all my parties at the lake!" It would be perfect actually, plenty for everybody to drink, and if you got hungry you could easily just grab a drunken fish out of the water, err, wine... it would even be pre-marinated!

We also see Jesus hanging out with a crowd of people every parent wants their teenagers to stay away from: prostitutes, thieves, and the like. In fact, He even hung out with them so much He was accused of being a drunken glutton! "For John came neither eating nor drinking, and they say, 'He has a demon!' The Son of Man came eating and drinking, and they say, 'Behold, a gluttonous man and a drunkard, a friend of tax collectors and sinners!' Yet wisdom is vindicated by her deeds." (Matthew 11:18, 19)

That verse is Jesus, Himself quoting the Pharisees, so He is acknowledging that He really does party with these sorts. So far, this personality of God is not really measuring up to what we would expect based on the way most churches would have us believe and how they would have us live. I wonder if other parents ever told their kids to stay away from that Jesus boy. "He's a bad influence with His parties, long hair, and crazy friends."

At least He never lost His temper... well, except for the time in John, Chapter 2 where He went berserk in the Temple, flinging tables all over the place and whipping people with a hand-made whip! (Wouldn't *that* be a collector's item!) And yes, this story takes place right after He turned water into wine... maybe He had been so good for so long, He just had one bad day? Oh wait, there was also that time in Matthew, Chapter 21 where He got mad at a fig tree for not having any figs on it and cursed it so it died (even though it wasn't fig season). I think that if I went to an apple tree and got so mad at it that I poisoned it for not having any apples it would probably be frowned upon in our day and age.

But, we know for sure He never cheated anybody or stole, although there was a strange parable He told once about how shrewd a servant was for swindling his master out of a bunch of money in order to save his skin. (Luke 16: 1-8)

Okay, well, at least as far as we know He didn't smoke, dance, or going to "R" rated movies. The fact is that most of us look at Jesus living a saintly life through the lenses of religion, but if this guy were walking the earth today, He'd get thrown out of most churches, which is funny because it looks like He got thrown out of most churches in His day, too! It really makes me want to hang out with the guy! Clearly this was a man who knew how to have a good time!

How is it that the personality of the very God most churches say they want to worship would most likely get thrown out of those same churches? Perhaps we have failed to accurately capture the true personality of the God we try to worship.

2

Self-Discovery

It's 5:22 A.M.... on my day off. Ever have that happen? Wake up early on a day you're supposed to be able to sleep in? I wonder if Jesus ever had that experience? Going to bed on Friday night thinking, "Yes, tomorrow is the Sabbath, I get to sleep in!" Then He wakes up an hour and a half before the rooster starts crowing and just sits there. I wonder what He thought about during those times? One would think that the Son of God would have a fair amount on His mind. What topics would occupy the thoughts of such an individual during the quiet hours? Did He ever try to remember life before His birth? *Could* He remember life before His birth? I wonder how much Christ really knew about who He was?

When we are born, we have no idea who we are, we have to learn how to walk, how to talk, how to dress ourselves. We have to learn about our culture, our family history, and our traditions, as we set sail on a journey of self-discovery. Did Jesus have to do the same thing? Was He simply born with a bunch of divine knowledge or did He have to discover it for Himself?

I really don't know, but there is a part of me that would like to believe He can relate to us in the journey of learning who we are. One thing is clear: Jesus gained a sense of who He was pretty early. We see a story in Luke, Chapter 2, where Jesus, at the age of twelve, gets separated from His parents while traveling back from the Passover Celebration in Jerusalem. The caravan is well on its way and His parents, no doubt thinking He's playing with some other kids along the journey, notice He hasn't been around for over a day! After frantically checking with everyone else in their group, they head back to Jerusalem. (I'm amused by the idea of random people coming up to Mary and Joseph and asking, "Have you found Jesus?" But I digress.) So, as I just mentioned, Luke writes they had been traveling over a day before they noticed Him missing. I'm guessing they probably traveled back a little faster, but I think it's safe to assume it probably took close to a day to get back. Then Luke writes that they spent three more days looking for Him before they found Him in the Temple courts! So, it's possible during this whole ordeal that Jesus was missing for up to five days!

My kids aren't teenagers yet, but I really don't like it when they are taught this story in Sunday School. The last thing I want them to put together is that Jesus was sinless and Jesus didn't think to check in with his parents for five days; therefore, not checking in with your parents is not a sin. Of course, if my kids ever do try and pull this one I'll be sure to point out that if they want to test that theory they had better be in a church when I find them because they are going to need a lot of witnesses!

But once Jesus is found and recovers from His mother slapping Him upside the back of the head, (it's in there but you have to go to the Greek to find it) He simply asks why they didn't think to look for Him in His "Father's house?" (Luke 2:49) The point in all of this is we can be certain that by the age of twelve, Jesus knew who His Father was. It's also clear He had a prodigy-like understanding of the scriptures for a child His age, or any age for that matter, and the teachers in the temple were blown away by this kid.

The question is, was He drawing on pre-incarnate knowledge from when He existed as "God", or did He have to learn all of this just like a regular person would have to? My guess here, or maybe just my hope, is that for Jesus to fully relate to us and our plight He would have had to learn who He was just like all the rest of us.

So, how would He have gone about doing this? Well, I'm guessing His parents probably shared with Him the remarkable story of His birth, how they were visited by an angel and how Mary was still a virgin, although she probably spared that part until He was old enough to have the birds and the bee's talk. How confusing would that be for a kid, huh?

Imagine that conversation:

Jesus: "Mommy, where do babies come from?"

Mary: "Well, honey, when a man and woman really love each other they get married and then, well… actually, look, you see what those two cats over there are doing?" Blah, blah, blah… and that's where babies come from."

Jesus: blink, blink… "EEEEHHHHHUUUUU, that's gross! So when I was born that's what you and Dad had to do?! I'm NEVER going to do that!"

Mary: "Well, actually no, you were a little different. With you, God just put you in my tummy."

Jesus: "Wait, so you and dad didn't do that?"

Mary: "No… not with you."

Jesus: "So God just puts babies in mommies' tummies?"

Mary: "No."

Jesus: "But He put me in your tummy."

Mary: "Yes."

Jesus: "I'm really confused."

Clearly I've gotten off track here, but the point I was trying to make is that there is no doubt that Mary would have shared with Jesus the story of His birth, which by its very nature was quite remarkable and was a fulfillment of scripture. Imagine the impact that would have on a kid as Mary and Joseph take Jesus to church and they open up a scroll and the Rabbi begins to read, "Therefore the Lord Himself will give you a sign: Behold, a virgin will be with child and bear a son, and she will call His name Immanuel." (Isaiah 7:14) Each time He goes to church He hears more and more passages that foretell the birth of the Messiah. I can imagine that reading about yourself in the scriptures would probably drive you to want to know as much as you possibly could about them. Think about how much more interesting the scriptures would be if there were parts that were directly about you, your future, and who you were destined to be? That would probably create a near obsession with reading them. Is that why He knew them so well? Did He know the scriptures with such precision simply because He was God or was it perhaps more human than that? Perhaps He knew them so well because He was curious, because, like any of us, He longed to discover who He really was. Perhaps on those early mornings when He couldn't sleep He would light a lamp, pull out a scroll, and continue searching, learning His own story.

How hard must it have been for Him to read passages like this from the book of Psalms: "For dogs have surrounded me; A band of evildoers has encompassed me; They pierced my hands and my feet. I can count all my bones. They look, they stare at me; They divide my garments among them, And for my clothing they cast lots." (Psalm 22:16-18) Or this one out of Isaiah: "But He was pierced through for our transgressions, He was crushed for our iniquities; The chastening for our well-being fell upon Him, And by His scourging we are healed. All of us like sheep have gone astray, Each of us has turned to his own way; But the LORD has caused the iniquity of us all to fall on Him." (Isaiah 53:5, 6)

I wonder how old Jesus was when He first saw a crucifixion and suddenly put together what those verses meant? Imagine the pit He must have felt in His stomach. Imagine how desperate He must have felt to search the Scriptures to see if He had missed something? He may have thought, "Maybe these passages are talking about someone else." Imagine the stress of having to come to grips with these things? It had to have been awful.

As Jesus got older it was quite apparent that He knew He was here to be a sacrifice. Could coming to terms with this have been part of the reason He took off into the wilderness by Himself for 40 days after John the Baptist left no doubt as to His identity at His baptism? I wonder how He interpreted the Passover story? What did He think every time He saw a lamb sacrificed? Recorded centuries before, there was that strange story in Genesis where God asked Abraham to sacrifice his son, Isaac. People had been doing their best to interpret that story for 2,000 years, trying to figure out what God was doing to Abraham. But I wonder if Jesus saw it differently? Was it obvious to Him what the symbolism was of God asking the founding father of the Jews to sacrifice his son? I wonder how often Jesus sat silently in church as some Rabbi preached on this topic, His mind a thousand miles away, pondering the true meaning of the passage the teachers thought they knew so well?

This actually explained for me a point of confusion about Jesus that I had carried for a long time. I never understood why in the Garden of Gethsemane Jesus prayed to God for another way. It makes sense why He wouldn't want to go through with being crucified, but I didn't know where He would have drawn the hope that there was possibly a way out. That is until my dear friend, Father Mike, pointed out that perhaps somewhere in the back of Jesus' mind He was clinging to an ancient story of an angel who appeared at the last second to save a boy who was about to be sacrificed.

All of those passages that indicated that the Messiah was to die as a sacrifice, all of the symbolism, everything pointing toward His hopeless demise... except one—one story that left just a sliver of hope that perhaps He could be spared. What torment, what anguish. Or, perhaps that story actually helped to provide Him with hope. After all, if Jesus really did have to learn all these things then He also would have had to learn that the Messiah would be raised up by God on the third day. If you remember, it took Abraham three days to get to the location of Isaac's sacrifice, which means the angel appeared and saved Isaac on the third day. Jonah was in the belly of the great fish three days.

Imagine if Jesus had to learn that God would save Him on the third day. Imagine the leap of faith He was taking in trusting that His interpretation of the scriptures was correct when every other teacher in His life saw them differently. Yes, perhaps the story of Isaac's salvation on the third day is what helped Him face His ordeal and gave Him the faith to trust that He, too, would be saved on the third day. Isn't it interesting? An angel proclaimed Isaac was saved and it was an angel that rolled the stone away to proclaim that the tomb was empty that first Easter morning. In fact, was it not

Jesus, Himself Who appeared after His resurrection to His followers on the road to Emmaus in Luke, Chapter 24, and used the Scriptures to explain all the things that were to happen to the Messiah?

Isn't it interesting that Jesus didn't just start sharing a bunch of divine wisdom with them, information that only He was privy to as God, but information that was right there for anyone to see, the very scriptures?! The knowledge was there for the taking for anyone who had eyes to see and ears to hear. Did Jesus really predict as much as we think He did? Or was He just a lot more in tune with what was right there in front of Him?

Perhaps that was the source of so much of Jesus' knowledge. Perhaps, like us, He also had to do a great deal of searching through external sources to learn who He was. And like the rest of us, He knew fully, perhaps better than anybody, what it's like to have to trust God with an uncertain future.

3

Adorable

"You will never amount to shit!"

The words hung in the air for a few moments before the exasperated mother stood up with a beet-red face and tearing eyes. Trembling with anger, she rose from her seat, opened the door to my office, and walked out, leaving her son sitting across from me with a blank look on his face. I could tell from his hollowed expression that he had heard these words a thousand times before. As the door closed with a thud behind her, the teenage boy looked at me and exclaimed, "See, that's how she always talks to me."

Ironically, he seemed to have immediately forgotten the fact that he had just unleashed a profanity-laced tirade at his mother prior to her proclamation of his future chances at success. This desperate mother had come to me seeking counsel regarding the behavior issues she was having with her boy. She had already shared about how he would not listen to her, how he was coming home whenever he wanted, and how he was so belligerent to her. I knew she hadn't meant what she had said, but it was already too late, the words had been said, the damage was done.

As I spoke to the son for awhile, he expressed that there was no motivation for him to behave because he knew his mother didn't like him anyway. He felt he had been replaced by her latest boyfriend, a guy that he loathed. He shared how he longed to go and live with his father, a man he barely knew, as his parents had split when he was a baby. I asked him if he had a good rapport with his father and he honestly replied that he had only met his dad on a handful of occasions, but anything had to be better than what he was experiencing right now.

This was a difficult situation for both the son and the mother, and it's hard to say where the breakdown first started. Was it with the mother or the son? Either way, one thing that I've learned is that when a child lashes out at a parent with profanities, it's painful, but when the parent responds the same way, it is downright devastating to the child, inflicting severe damage that will not soon be forgotten.

The desire to be loved is a basic one. Each of us long to be loved by someone and in our early years the people we crave it from most tend to be our parents. It is our parents who have the power to first instill in us the idea that we are lovable; and unfortunately, it is also our parents who can first instill in us the idea that we are not lovable at all. The wounds that can occur during these fragile years are ones we can carry with us for the rest of our lives. They can drive us into all kinds of self-destructive behaviors, seeking the love we have been ingrained to believe we don't have or don't deserve.

Insecurities about love can ironically even undermine marriages as people continue to seek confirmation of love from one who has already committed an entire life to them, constantly pushing them to prove their love over and over until they drive their spouse insane with pestering. This can also seep into our spiritual lives as we struggle with the idea that God could ever love us. We can push ourselves to our wit's end trying to be "good enough" to earn God's love, constantly trying to reassure ourselves of His adoration and our salvation. That, of course, is if we haven't already thrown up our hands and given up on a silent God who hasn't jumped through our hoops well enough to earn our reciprocated affection.

One of the things about Christ that is extremely clear from the Gospels is that He was completely comfortable with the idea that God thoroughly adored Him. Over and over we see Him make reference to this: "Just as the Father has loved Me, I have also loved you; abide in My love." (John 15:9)

"For this reason the Father loves Me, because I lay down My life so that I may take it again." (John 10:17)

"… and behold, a voice out of the heavens said, 'This is My beloved Son, in whom I am well-pleased.'" (Matthew 3:17)

This is a rather important aspect to grasp from Christ because He demonstrates something that most of us struggle with. He makes it very clear that God loves us, but for some reason we don't seem to embrace this concept as well as He did. Sure, it's easy to point out that since Christ never sinned it was a lot easier for Him to accept God's love, but I'm now starting to wonder if that was the point. If the reason God loved Jesus so much was because He was sinless, then Jesus Himself would have known that God's love was conditional on the fact that He remained perfect. That's a lot of pressure! And to be quite frank, it's not real love. So, if God loved Jesus because He really just loved Him, then the fact that Christ was sinless couldn't have even been a factor in the equation. God would have loved Christ even if He had sinned!

So, what can we take away from this? Well, when we break it down to the most basic premise, Jesus was a regular guy who completely embraced the fact that God's love for Him was completely genuine and real. The fact is that God's love for us is just as intense. The difference is that we simply have a hard time embracing the idea.

A lot of us question how we could be loved or how God could love us, and as a result we tend to create our own barriers with Him. Many times our ability to accept love is also dependent upon how lovable we believe ourselves to be. When we don't feel lovable, we can easily become suspicious of any love directed toward us because we don't feel like we deserve it. This is a very human trait because many of us have somehow developed this ability to qualify love. The fact that we can even attribute words like "deserve" in talking about love clearly shows that we have created an environment where love must be something that is earned. A situation where some sort of strange threshold must be attained to validate the love we are receiving.

It often seems we live in a world of flattery, one where people might compliment us for things that aren't really true. Someone might tell us that we did a good job at something when we know we did not, causing us to call their sincerity into question. Yes, I suspect we've all experienced it and we hate the feeling we get when someone is being insincere.

When we know the kind of people we are, when we struggle with loving ourselves then it can be very difficult to buy into the idea that God really does love us significantly with a love that doesn't have to be earned. Again, our barriers are not because of God, they are because of us. They are grounded in our insecurities and they make it difficult to accept the unconditional love that He offers.

There is a natural fear of being wounded when it comes to giving and receiving love, and sometimes when we decide to offer our love to another there can be pressure to crave love in return, and that creates vulnerability. We tend to struggle with the idea of being vulnerable because being vulnerable is risky and can lead to great pain.

But Jesus somehow as a regular guy, grasped the concept that the love of God is a divine love, it transcends all things, and is blind to our failures. It is not affected by our performance in this life; it is solely based on who we are as His children. Jesus knew what it was to be human. Jesus knew that being human was being created in God's image. Just as Christ was a divine individual, we, too, are divine individuals. Just as Christ was the Son of God, we, too, are sons and daughters of God. This confidence of God's love for Him was not reserved only for Jesus; it is for all of us. We are all divine creatures and we have just as much authority as Christ did to claim and embrace that love for us.

During my years in ministry, I dealt with a great number of people who had struggled with their failures. Instead of simply accepting God's love for them, they embraced the feelings of guilt for their past indiscretions. One such story was about a young lady named Rachel. Rachel came into our church one day completely out of the blue. She was very upset and seemed awkward even being here. When she entered, she was met warmly by our greeters and eventually found her way to the Welcome Center in the lobby. She was in her early- to mid-20's so when the lady running the welcome center realized Rachel was struggling, she came and got me, as I was the pastor to that age group at the time. I asked Rachel if she needed to talk to someone and she said she would like to. I grabbed a tissue box and we headed off to my office. Once there, she sat down in a chair and began to sob quietly for a few moments. After she gathered herself a bit she began to share with me that she had been a "Christian" all of her life. She said she was familiar with the Bible and knew it quite well. She said that when she was in high school she attended her youth group and was basically a good little girl, but once she graduated and got out on her own she gradually stopped attending church and eventually began to explore the world she had so devotedly kept herself from in her youth.

She started to attend the parties and experiment with alcohol and marijuana, she became sexually active and eventually found she really didn't like the idea of casual sex. She expressed how hard it was not to feel betrayed when a guy would show so much interest in her only to wish her well and disappear the next morning. She would get upset at herself for getting upset as she knew going into these situations they were probably only going to be a one night stand. Although it seemed fun in the moment, the next day she would always feel hollow, wishing that there was something deeper to her life and her relationships. She lamented that she never really knew if a guy truly liked her or if he just wanted to have sex with her. As a result, she began to wonder how likable she would be if sex were not part of the equation?

Her mind began to run with the idea that she really wasn't likeable at all, and that the only reason guys really paid attention to her was to get something else. That's when it all started to crumble on her. She began to feel the weight of all she had learned in her youth about God and Jesus. She remembered all of the lessons about avoiding sin and staying pure until marriage and as it all crashed down on her she felt more and more worthless. With her hands in her face and a soaked tissue between them, she expressed,

"I don't know if any of the guys I've been with really loved me, and now, because of all the things I've done, nobody at any church will love me either. I know God forgives and everything, but I just feel so guilty."

Rachel had learned her lesson. She had reached out touched the hot stove and gotten burned, and now she was paying for her mistakes twice by subjecting herself to such tremendous guilt.

The story of Rachel really represents many conversations I've had over the years with numerous people. People who have sat in my office and continue to beat themselves up after having been assured they were already forgiven. One of the most common responses I have received has been that they don't want to let themselves off too easily. How many of us can relate to that? You know the scenario, the one where someone wrongs us and we try to make them live in that guilt until we feel their penitence has been completed. Then once we are satisfied with the amount of suffering they have experienced, we finally let them off the hook. But we don't only do this to others; we do it to ourselves. It's almost as if there is a certain satisfaction that comes with self-deprecation. But fortunately, with every sin comes an opportunity for the sinner to learn a lesson. When the lesson is really learned, then guilt becomes unnecessary and self-destructive. It doesn't matter if the guilt lasts a minute or a year, it accomplishes nothing. It's the lesson learned that's most important.

Going back to the stove analogy, when I was growing up, the old ranch house we lived in didn't have heat. Everything was warmed by a couple of stone fireplaces. I remember one time we were sitting in the kitchen eating and my little sister came in crying with her index finger sticking out and a small blister on the end. When my parents asked what had happened she cried out that she had touched one of the "red things" in the fire place. That "red thing," of course, was a small coal that was left over from the fire the night before. I can imagine the curiosity in her little mind, sitting there on the floor, looking into the fire place and staring at that enticing, little, glowing orb. She may have thought, "What a pretty color it is; I wonder if I could make it into a glow in the dark earring or something?" She had probably learned somewhere that those things are hot, but this one didn't look very hot. It's just sitting there in the ashes, no flames or anything abound it. "I'll bet this one has probably cooled off enough that I can pick it up. In fact, this is so pretty, I think I'll just take it in and show it to everybo.... AAAAHHHHHHH!!!!!!!!" Well, my sister was pretty young when that happened and as far as I know, she hasn't intentionally picked up another coal since then. With a seared finger she learned her lesson and she learned it immediately.

But, imagine if she hadn't touched the coal. What might have happened then? Perhaps she would have sat by that fire every day for weeks wondering what it would be like to pick up one of those beautiful coals. Oh, she would have known she wasn't supposed to, and as an obedient little girl she would have resisted the urge, but in the mean time she might have spent hours, looking longingly at it, wondering how amazing that enticing little gem would be to hold. Perhaps she would have been obedient in not touching it, but she may have wasted weeks or months of her life away, sitting in front of it, longing for it. In that situation, which would have been worse for her? To have touched the coal, been burned, but then to have learned a dramatic lesson and never be tempted again, or to sit in constant temptation, wasting part of her life away wondering?

A strong argument could probably be made for either, but there really is something to be said for the lessons we learn from our mistakes. Now, please understand I'm not condoning that one go out and engage in irresponsible debauchery in order to "learn lessons," but I am saying that if the sin has already been committed and the lesson has been learned, then guilt at that point is really counter-productive. One doesn't need to sit and continue to beat him or herself up for a mistake once the lesson has been learned. Imagine if my sister continually apologized to my parents to this day for her indiscretion of picking up that coal? Imagine how my parents would have felt about that? They would simply tell her she learned her lesson so forget about it and stop beating herself up. In fact, they probably would have told her that an hour after the event.

Why would God be any different? Some of us still need to embrace the love that He is extending and not place our own emotional roadblocks in the way or project our own feelings onto God. The fact is that most of us will beat ourselves up until we feel we have suffered enough, and when we do, it is still more about us than it is about God. When we, like Christ, can fully embrace the idea that we are completely and totally adorable to God no matter what, it becomes much easier to not only love and forgive ourselves but for us to do the same for others.

Each of us has met people who just rub us the wrong way, those people who may be perfectly fine individuals but for some reason we just can't seem to jive with them. They have that habit, or a tendency that we can't relate to. Perhaps we simply have nothing in common with them.

Do you suppose Jesus ever came across people like this, people He just had a hard time hanging out with? Cough... Pharisees... cough... cough.... How was He able to still find ways to love people like this? I think there are instances where we have to take the time to go deeper than just the surface issues with people we don't like.

The fact is that at our core, all of us are pretty much the same. We all want to be loved, we all are insecure, and we all have basic, raw, and primal emotions that make us human.

One of the biggest revelations I have had as a police officer was when I've made the connection that the biggest difference between me and the people I arrested was that I was lucky enough to be born into a different situation.

Had I been born to a drug addicted prostitute, my life would probably have been extremely different. In fact, when I've learned the stories behind many of the people I've dealt with, I've discovered the biggest difference between them and me was simply that I was raised in a different set of circumstances.

This fact has really changed my heart as to how I treat people. When I began to see them less as screw ups, losers, and derelicts and began to see them as myself under different circumstances, I eventually got to the place where I could actually like people that were cursing me and spewing hatred, simply because I could still see myself in them. I learned to start viewing people not so much as who they were but more as what they had been through.

I imagine Jesus was the ultimate expert at this; He was able to peer into the darkest of hearts and still connect with the morsel of humanity that remained, and that was what He fell in love with, the humanity within us all: the part of Him in everybody else. When others failed to see themselves as adorable to the Father, He simply did it for them.

4

Salvation

When I was seven years old, I accepted Christ into my heart as my Lord and Savior. At least, that is the age I decided to settle on as the age of my salvation. The truth was that by the age of seven I must have accepted Christ into my heart about twenty or thirty times. I had been assured by my Sunday School teachers that once I was saved I was always saved, but I wasn't so sure. I knew I had said the right words, but I never felt "saved." Although, I guess I didn't really know what it felt like to be "saved."

I knew I didn't really feel different than I did before I said the prayer, so my assumption was that something didn't work. Surely being "saved" would be accompanied by some sort of wonderful feeling, a vision from God, perhaps a choir of angels singing, a toaster oven, something,... ANYTHING. I was never completely sure about whether I was really saved once I said those prayers. I was taught that in order to truly be saved one had to "believe" in Jesus. I struggled with this because I was also taught that if I had the faith of a mustard seed then I should have been able to move mountains. Once I quickly learned that I was unable to move those mountains, or even turn on a light without clapping for that matter, I doubted if I was really saved at all.

I remember sitting on the hill above our house looking out at the mountains of Southern Arizona and attempting to cast different ones into the ocean. Of course, as a child, I never really thought about the fact that there were very likely people on those mountains who probably would not have appreciated that particular prayer being answered affirmatively. I can imagine a retired couple sitting in their cabin enjoying the fruits of their life labors waking up in the morning and seeing fish swimming by their kitchen windows as the result of a punk kid a hundred miles away testing out his new faith.

But if I truly did "believe," then there should have been some miracles happening, right? Since there weren't, it was clear to me that I must not have really believed and was, therefore, not saved. This was very troubling to me. Even after the age of seven, I still continued accepting Christ now and then just to be safe, but when people would stand up and give their testimonials in church or at camp, I noticed many could actually give the day they were saved. It was such a profoundly dramatic event in their lives that they remembered the actual day! I couldn't remember the day, but I specifically remember reciting one of my prayers when I was seven; therefore, seven was the age I used from then on.

From as far back as I recall my biggest motivation for accepting Christ was that I was very certain I did not want to go to hell. Even as a child, I was very aware of the terrors that awaited those who failed to accept Jesus into their hearts, and I didn't even attend a hell-fire and brimstone-toting church! I feared death. Growing up on a ranch, death was something I became familiar with at a fairly young age. Be it cats, dogs, cattle, horses, or hamsters, there was always some sort of creature that was dying around the property.

As a result, it didn't take me long to recognize this same fate would someday await me. I wanted to make sure when it came, I was squared away with God.

Other than hell, I had another fear about death. What if all this Bible stuff wasn't true? What if I just lived this entire life and at the end, we simply died and there was nothing? A fear of death leading to nothingness was almost as terrifying as an eternal hell. I was fearful I would be forever conscience in a world of nothing, no light, no sound, no body, no people, not even crickets. Kinda like being stuck in outer space minus the stars to give light. I know I probably sound like this traumatized me, and maybe it did, but it really was a huge concern for me. And apparently it wasn't just a fear for me. I have since learned that I was definitely not alone in those childhood fears. During a recent radio interview the host shared with me the story of her father who had been a devout Christian his entire life, yet on his deathbed confessed that he feared he was not "saved." As she told the brief story, I began to feel my temperature rise as my heart broke for both her and her father. How do we escape this genuine fear that can torment us from the cradle to the deathbed?

The Human Side of Christ

    Then as I got older, I eventually got to wondering if Jesus ever struggled with any of those concerns. Naturally, I would assume the idea of going to hell or failing to attain heaven were probably not too big on His mind. What a lucky guy! Here I was as a child having nightmares about heaven and hell and whether or not I was going to make it to heaven, while He as a child of the same age would have been able to lay His head down every night and at the very least, know that as the Son of God, He had absolutely nothing to worry about. In fact, if the fear of what happens to us after we die was not something He ever dealt with, then in a way, He missed out a bit on a basic human concern.

    So the next question would have to be: what *did* Jesus think about? As a model human, shouldn't we be able to base our entire lives around Him and the way He lived His? I'm guessing Jesus never really worried about going to hell as a result of His lack of faith in God. I'm also guessing He wasn't worried about reaching that mysterious threshold of what was required to get into heaven. So if He wasn't worried about heaven and hell, then what was He worried about? The only thing I can really speculate is that if He wasn't all that concerned about His afterlife, then He probably spent most of His time thinking about His current life! Think about it, when we make the highest priority of this life to make sure things are okay in the next life, then isn't the next life our main focus? And if the afterlife is our main focus, then doesn't that diminish some of the significance of this life? After all, I do remember Jesus commenting about living life in the present: "So do not worry about tomorrow; for tomorrow will care for itself. Each day has enough trouble of its own." (Matthew 6:34)

If Jesus didn't worry about heaven and hell, I wonder if we really need to worry about them that much? If my main motivation for living the life that Jesus demonstrated is simply to make sure I get into heaven or perhaps more importantly, to make sure I don't go to hell then are my motives really all that pure? To be honest, those motives sound rather selfish. It would seem strangely ironic for me to live a sacrificial life that is dedicated to others if my main focus was really to ensure that I ended up in a safe place after I die. So the conclusion that I have drawn from the example Jesus set in the way He lived is that this life must contain profound significance in and of itself. What if the main goal of this life is a lot more than just a trial run for the next life? Then what could it be?

5

Life to the Full

"So do not worry about tomorrow; for tomorrow will care for itself. Each day has enough trouble of its own."
(Matthew 6:34)

Life is fascinating, isn't it? I find it interesting to think about the fact that scientists tell us that the world and the universe have been around for millions and billions of years. All that time, a whole bunch of stuff happened—stars, planets, earthquakes, dinosaurs, wars, kingdoms, civilizations—all kinds of events took place that I missed. Then, all of a sudden, without any warning or request, here I am. I didn't even do anything to get here.

My earliest memories are of being a young child; before that a hazy fog of mystery that is only explained by family pictures and stories told by my parents. Sometimes I look around at other people in this world, especially those born with disabilities, and ponder how they had just as little control over their physical situations as I had in being lucky enough to have a body that is healthy and works. So many preset factors had sculpting influences on my life, including my gender, my race, even my height, weight, hair and eye color. Where I was born, when I was born, all factors we have absolutely no control over, yet have profound impact on our lives and our experiences in this life.

Then, just as we miraculously entered this world we will one day leave it and be gone forever. Out of the universe's billions of years of existence, we show up for a few moments and then leave. Like a vapor. (Seems like I've heard that one somewhere before.) It's as if the universe and all its splendors are constants and, for a few moments, we get to step into this realm with bodies as our vessels to experience what it has to offer, then as quickly as we got here, we are gone. Kind of like taking a brief submarine ride in the ocean: the quality of the experience is related to the capabilities of the machine.

When we break life down to its most basic form, it is really only a collection of experiences: information being collected and stored from moment to moment, every second containing its own little treasure of sights, smells, tastes, sounds, and feelings. With the gifts of five senses, we process the world around us and interpret as much of it as we can. We use these senses to identify people, places, and things. Each sense, when in balance, has the power to create incredible pleasure and when overwhelmed can inflict severe pain, all of them working together, every second of every day, to comprise this thing we call life.

Yet, as special and as wonderful as it is, most of us sleepwalk right through it. We spend our days in repetitive cycles, missing out on the miracles around us. One of the most amazing experiences of my life was after my first child was born. I remember walking down a street with him as a toddler and we came across an ant colony. He pointed it out to me and I acknowledged it before telling him to come along. I looked back and he was still fascinated by it. That's when it suddenly hit me... he'd never seen this before! I was actually witnessing someone experiencing something for the very first time. That day changed how I viewed each of my children. Each one entered the world as a clean slate, an empty hard drive waiting to be filled with experiences, ready to pay attention to each little miracle they come across, ready to remind me how to look at the world, and re-appreciate all the things I've since taken for granted.

Sometimes I can still go there. When I focus, I can remember playing with my trucks in my sand box, distracted by birds chirping, and bugs crawling. Not once did I think about retirement, or a house payment, or a work deadline. I just lived. But then over time, I became conditioned by this world and began to live less and less in the "now" and more and more in the "when." At first it was "someday when" and then over time it was balanced by "back when." But so seldom was it "now." "Now" is something I've had to re-teach myself.

I wonder, "Did Jesus ever struggle with that mindset? Did He ever catch himself overlooking a moment? Or was He so in tune with life that He possessed, or at least cultivated, that He had the ability to enjoy every moment for what it was? When did He first grasp the idea He shared with us about not worrying about tomorrow? Not to worry about where we would get our food or clothing and to rely on God for our provisions?"

Whether we think about it or not, this life really is temporary but I'm afraid that most of us live our lives as if they are eternal. I've heard people say things like, "Live each day as if it were your last." But I have to be honest when I look at it that way, I get depressed. I think if I knew I only had 24 hours left, I'd be a little down. But when I think about existence, all we really have is right now. The past is gone forever, sealed in the unchanging vault of time. And the future doesn't exist yet. Right now is all we have, right this second. We have a couple of choices as to how we want to spend right now. We can ignore it by focusing on other things, we can loath it, or we can embrace it. Savoring it and enjoying it for exactly what it is: an experience. Whether good or bad, it is still an experience that is sculpting our lives and for that reason can be savored as such.

Life is perhaps the most unique thing in the entire universe. It's possible that we might be the only planet in the entire cosmos where it exists. At the very least, we know it's extremely rare, as scientists are constantly finding new planets around distant stars and seldom do they ever show the promise of containing the circumstances for sustaining life.

The only avenue to experience anything is through life. Be it pain or pleasure, happiness or sadness, fear or contentment, they can only be experienced by a living creature. And they can only be fully appreciated by a living creature that is self-aware, which is even more rare. In that regard, even suffering can be appreciated because suffering can't even be known by anything other than an entity experiencing the miracle of life. Perhaps living life to the full is not just about trying to do as many things possible with each moment of life. Perhaps it is also about learning to appreciate everything every moment has to offer. Whether the mundane wait in line at the Department of Motor Vehicles, or the excitement of a roller coaster, the pleasure of a beach vacation, or the suffering of cancer, each are lived, each are rare, and perhaps all can be appreciated for what they really are: experiences solely available to a living creature.

Jesus was so profoundly right when He told us not to worry; not one situation in the history of the world has ever been solved by worrying. What is, is, whether we worry about it or not, so we might as well let go of the worry. Clearly this is much easier said than done, but such is the case with most things in life that are worthwhile.

As unique as life is, I suppose that perhaps someday we will find it elsewhere, out there in this vast expanse, but I'm pretty sure even if we do it will be in limited amounts. We can look no further than our own solar system to see that. So out of the trillions and trillions of atoms that exist in this entire universe, we have one planet where a few of them have clumped together into piles of molecular star dust that have the ability to see, hear, taste, touch, and smell. And each of us enjoys the incredibly unique experience of being one of those collections of atoms.

Perhaps the rarest thing in all of existence is a living being and we have the honor of being one of them. That's one reason why suicide doesn't make much sense to me. As mentioned earlier, life is a collection of experiences, and death is the only experience that each and every one of us is guaranteed to experience. If life is about experiencing as much as possible, why do we need to rush into ending it? If we really are the rarest thing around, and it is only a temporary experience, why cut it short? I can understand those who are suffering or in great pain perhaps reaching the end of their rope, but there are still so many more who make this huge decision for reasons that will forever be a mystery to their loved ones. Their actions are never fully understood by those they leave behind.

Jesus mastered living right now, and extracted every ounce of life from every second. He had the ability to appreciate every moment as it came. He never rushed to anything, even to heal people. He didn't create artificial deadlines. He was never "too busy" to stop and help the next person in need, to the point that it had to be very frustrating for those around Him—especially those waiting on Him to heal someone before death took them.

Jesus was so comfortable and so in tune with God, He didn't worry about time tables. He would heal the person when He got there. If they died first, He would raise them. Because of this profound connection with God, a deadline was never a deadline for Jesus; it was only a line, an illusion created by man.

This allowed Him to live life on His terms. He moved and acted deliberately with every encounter. Nothing forced His hand; nothing caused Him to stray from His path because He was not distracted by the pressures of this life. I'm curious if one of the things that may have helped Him with this might have been the understanding that He was to be crucified. If it were possible to know how and when we were going to die, perhaps we wouldn't be in such a rush to do anything, especially if that death was to be by torture and to occur at a fairly young age. Were that the case, I suppose I wouldn't want a second to pass of which I didn't take advantage. The thing is, each of our lives is temporary, and none of us are guaranteed a peaceful passing in our sleep. We all know what awaits us, we just don't know how or when.

What we do know is what we have right now. Let's savor the moment and let go of worrying about tomorrow... it won't do much good anyway.

6

Denial or Self-Denial?

*"The richest man is not he who has the most,
but he who needs the least."*

~ Unknown

With burning legs and gasps for air I took the last few steps to climb up and over the ridge. It was our third day in the wilderness and we hadn't seen a soul outside of our four-man group. Today's journey was short, only three miles, but it had taken several hours as we had ascended over 2,000 feet in elevation. I walked over to a downed tree laying in the grassy meadow surrounded by the white bark of Aspen trees and slung off the heavy pack. I had arrived before the rest of the group, which left me an hour to myself in a saddle between two mountains.

At 10,000 feet the air was cool and clean and the forest seemed alive as leaves erupted in applause every time the breeze would make its way through the branches. I pulled out some trail mix and sat down in the lush cushion of green grass, surrounded by dandelions and colorful wild flowers as the cotton seed pods from the trees drifted down like snow. As I munched on my snack I realized that this was perhaps the most relaxed I had been in years. I remember musing at how odd that was. Here I sat on a remote mountain, miles away from civilization. No roads, no traffic, no cell phones, just miles of forest in every direction. Everything I needed to survive was strapped in the backpack that lay next to me. In that moment I realized just how little I needed in this life. All the material pursuits seemed silly to me: the house, the car, the job. My life at home now seemed extravagant and excessive compared to this moment. From here there was nothing to worry about. In this remote location I was so far away from everything. I was helpless to have any impact on anything that might occur back home. And it was in that complete and total helplessness that I found a profound peace. It was a realization that even when I am home, I still have very little control over so much of my life. One of the reasons I love to go backpacking for several days at a time is because it is in moments like these out in the wilderness that I realize just how much stress with which I constantly live. It's not until the stress is gone that I'm aware it's even there to begin with. It is when I'm out there with almost nothing that I am reminded how much more, less can be.

I have to believe that if He had wanted to, Jesus could have been a very wealthy man. After all, I'm sure people would have been more than willing to pay a small fee for a miracle. He could have charged admission to hear Him speak or He could have written a few scrolls while on His three-year circuit and sold them to a publisher if one existed. Prior to that, I'm sure He could have been an extremely successful carpenter. He was clearly brilliant enough to have done quite well for Himself with whatever He chose to do. So the question is… why didn't He pursue other endeavors?

Most of us would answer that He came here to do His Father's bidding, not to live a life of wealth and luxury, but one of humility and simplicity. As we read the Bible, we see the theme of simplicity is a rather prevalent concept, not one that was reserved solely for Christ. But have you ever wondered why? Why would God put us on this earth, which contains so many different ingredients for opulence and comfort if self-denial was the main theme?

The guy clearly had to live, and clearly had to support Himself during His life, so I think we would be naive in assuming He never had to earn a living. But where is the line between earning a living and building unnecessary wealth? Or is there such a thing as unnecessary wealth? After all, don't we need wealthy people to be able to give to the poor and support ministries? If everybody denied themselves everything then we wouldn't be much help to the needy, now would we? So, was Jesus' choice of self-denial just a ploy to intentionally add to His hardship on this earth, to suffer for God, or is it possible there was a more practical reason for His simplicity? To answer this, I think we need to first take an honest look at what the benefits are, if any, to living a life of maximum simplicity. If Jesus chose to give up everything, I think we would be insulting Him to imply that it was done merely to suffer. I'm not sure I see Him as a self-induced martyr, drawing attention to Himself because His life was "so hard."

The constant message Jesus proclaimed was freedom. So, I think it is important to look at every aspect of His life to see how each factor contributed to His absolute freedom as a human being. For most of us here in America, the idea of letting go of all of our possessions does not sound freeing at all. In fact, it seems quite the opposite! But think about this: Jesus never had to worry about locking the doors to His house, He never had to worry about thieves, He never worried if He left the stove on, if His insurance was paid up, or how much electricity He was using. He was free from having to make sure the cat was fed. He never worried about resale or stock market drops, or paying off the debt from the pool. He didn't have a television so He was free from being miserable all day after His favorite college football team lost... every other Saturday. He didn't have a smart phone so He didn't waste hours of His life sitting and waiting for little dots to move around a tiny screen giving Him game updates... only to be miserable for the rest of the day... after his team lost (not that this has ever been an issue for me of course... it's not like I'm some loser who gets overly upset about a bunch of 20-year-olds playing a game hundreds of miles from where I live).

He was able to live His life, completely free and unpossessed by possessions and their effects. If someone said, "Hey! Let's go to Jerusalem for the weekend," He could up and leave with no worries. In fact, it was Jesus Himself that said it is difficult for the rich to enter into the kingdom of God. (Luke 18:25) So if Jesus' main goal in life was to dwell in the "kingdom of God" then perhaps His way of life had nothing to do with self-denial, and had everything to do with self improvement.

Jesus was a free man, and I'd wager to say He was the freest man that ever lived. So if that was the case, then His choice to live on such meager means could not have been simply to suffer for no reason. If someone chooses to suffer pointlessly, then it's highly likely that their motives are simply to be a martyr. Pointless suffering doesn't equate to freedom; rather, to the opposite. Suffering viewed as self-imposed and pointless often leads to resentment. Have you ever met that Christian? The one who gives up everything to "live like Jesus" but in reality acts as if they drink lemon juice every morning? The one who makes a point of telling you all the things they can't do in life because it's "against their religion" or because "I am a Christian..."?

I have a hard time believing this is how Jesus walked around. As a Christian there have been many times in my life, especially during high school, when I would watch all the fun that my friends would have doing all the things that high school people do and secretly wish I could join them. There were times, before I understood the full benefits of how Christ lived, that I resented my inability to be able to do some of the things other people did. I really did feel like a martyr to my faith. I lived it out of obligation and fear, not out of freedom. You see, even though I did the "right" things, I never understood why they were the right things. I think Jesus lived the life He lived because He actually wanted to. I think He lived a life that brought Him the greatest amount of joy and freedom and that He did it willingly and enthusiastically, not begrudgingly as so many of us do.

So the true balance of freedom is found in living free from our possessions, not imprisoned by coveting what we wish we had or wish we could do. True freedom is living a life that pursues only that which is truly important.

7

The Broken Law

"Do not think that I came to abolish the Law or the Prophets;
I did not come to abolish but to fulfill."
(Matthew 5:17)

Law. What would society look like without it? Most would make a pretty strong case that without law society would be a chaotic mess of anarchy: people living as they pleased, fighting for whatever this earth has to offer. Vigilantism would rule the world.

Over the centuries mankind has displayed law is needed for us to live in a civilized, orderly manner. Law makes things predictable. Even in instances where laws are excessive and crippling to a society, order is still maintained. Man is a wild creature. Being wild is both our curse and our blessing as we have the ability to dream the impossible and take the risks to get there, but it is that same wild spirit that will also drive us to strike out against the confines of society and venture down our own road, living life as we see fit, no matter the cost to others.

There are those of us who have a hard time playing well with others and were it not for the coercive power of law, we would conduct ourselves in vastly different ways. For others, not even the rule of law keeps them in line.

One of the things that I find interesting is when people blend the idea of law with morality. How often have we heard someone make the point that they "haven't done anything illegal" when conducting themselves in a questionable manner. A great number of us are inherently obedient if we simply possess something or someone to obey. But when those coercers don't exist, it can get pretty wild. In fact we can look no further than the wild kingdom itself to see the results of a world without rules.

Animals are not governed by any sort of moral code; they simply do what it takes to survive. Animals live by instinct, reacting to urges that drive them into action. When they are hungry they are willing to eat almost anything that will satisfy that hunger. Male genders of many species will kill any other male if it perceives a threat to their dominion, even their own offspring. These actions are not done out of any sort of malicious intent; they are simply the result of the creature's natural instincts to survive. Essentially, all they are doing is looking out for number one.

When we look back through the history of mankind and some of the harms we have inflicted upon each other, we have at times demonstrated we are not much more advanced than the animal kingdom in some areas. History sadly records a number of instances where kings and dictators struck down their own flesh and blood if they saw them as threats to their rule. This is a pathetic testament to the fact that as advanced as man may seem in some areas, we are on par with the savagery of the animal kingdom in others. In fact, due to our ability to exercise preconceived malice in our actions, we can demonstrate behavior at levels far below our animal counterparts. At least they are acting out of instinct rather than direct intention.

When it comes down to the bare bones, almost all of the wrongs ever done by one person to another can be traced to the simple idea of putting one's self first. When I choose to steal from you, it is because I have determined that my desire for what you have is greater than your right to keep it. When I strike you in aggression it is because I have decided to place my desire to hurt you above your welfare. When I drive past that lady whose car has broken down on the freeway, I've decided that keeping my schedule is more important than helping her with her situation. We can look at a variety of situations, but for the most part when stripped down to the core of the issue it simply comes down to me putting myself, my needs, and my desires above you and yours. Thus, the grand invention of law. It's a treaty of sorts, an agreed upon social contract in which we trade some of our desires and hopes for the security of a civilized and orderly society. It does not cure every issue, but it does at least provide an alternative to chaos with a predictable framework in which society can function.

I find it interesting that Jesus made the statement that He did not come to "abolish" the Law because He constantly stirred controversy for violating the very same Law He wasn't seeking to abolish! In fact, right after Jesus made this declaration in Matthew, Chapter 5, He came out and said that you should love your enemy rather than extract an eye for an eye. At that time, an eye for an eye was the law and Jesus had just dismissed it. Now to be fair, it should be noted an "eye for an eye" was not that bad of a law for its time because it prevented people from extracting more than what was done to them. In a violent age where revenge was paid ten, twenty, or a hundred fold, "eye for an eye" limited the amount of punishment that could be demanded. Even so, Jesus took this law of justice and made it obsolete by calling people not to justice, but to love. He would "work" on the Sabbath. He was criticized because His disciples did not engage in proper ceremonial washings. When an adulterous woman was brought before Him to be stoned, He did not concede to the Law and allow her to be stoned even though that was what it demanded. For a guy who had no intention of "abolishing" the law, He certainly picked a number of very public times to violate it!

One consideration with law is that it doesn't only demand of us to live better than we might otherwise, it can also provide a ceiling in which people will do no more than what is required by law for others. The fact is Jesus could not abolish the Law because society was not, and still is not ready for such a thing. But perhaps the reason Jesus didn't need to live according to the Law is because He lived above it. Jesus lived His life by the code of loving others as He loved Himself. He loved everybody, even His enemies, and when you live a life like that, you don't need law. Law is needed to keep order, to prevent people from hurting or wronging one another. But for the one who lives by the law of love, there is no need for rules and regulations because that person will only do well for others.

If humanity ever wanted to experience utopia, we could do it in one second if everyone decided to love others as themselves. Laws would instantly be obsolete and unnecessary for mankind as we would not only be kind to each other, we would actively seek to do well for each other. If we could ever live by the code of love, there would no longer be a need for law.

When Jesus said He was here to fulfill the Law, He clearly didn't intend to follow every rule in the Law, because He didn't. So then what did He mean? What if He meant that by "fulfilling" the law He was here to fulfill the purpose or the intent of the law? After all, law exists so we will treat each other better, so if we took that concept all the way to its conclusion, the highest level would be to love each other. Jesus accomplished so much more than what can be done by just obeying the law. He soared way past its demands and requirements to something much higher. In most situations, when Jesus conducted Himself in a loving manner He was within the law; but occasionally, love would take Him beyond the law, and these were the instances where He "violated" or "broke" it. "Eye for an eye" is not loving my enemy, stoning the adulteress was not love. In these instances, I suspect Jesus violated the law of the day not because it went too far but because it didn't go far enough. I don't believe that Jesus was just trying to be defiant. Instead, He recognized that in these instances the law did not reach the threshold of love by which He lived His life, so as a result, rather than limiting Himself to what was "legal" and resting there, He stuck to His convictions and called His audiences to a better way.

The Apostle Paul summed it up best when he immortalized these ancient words: "But the fruit of the Spirit is love, joy, peace, patience, kindness, goodness, faithfulness, gentleness, self-control; against such things there is no law." (Galatians 5:22, 23)

8

Jesus and Sexuality

It was a warm sunny day on the beaches of San Diego. As was our tradition for a number of years we were vacationing in Southern California with dear friends of ours. Our kids had practically grown up together and for a week each summer we looked forward to the opportunity to hang out. We normally stayed in the sleepy beach town of Point Loma which was quiet during the summer as the local college students in the area were on vacation.

As least two to three days of our vacations would be spent on a beach under an umbrella, being lulled by the crashing waves and serenaded by the seagulls. On one such occasion, my buddy, Norm, and I had positioned our beach chairs in the sun, facing the waters, so we could keep an eye on our children while the wives sat a few feet away in the shade of the umbrellas chatting. Surprisingly, the beach was not as crowded as usual. Norm and I were in some sort of a profound conversation trying to solve the problems of the world when it suddenly happened. Two young ladies dressed in a pair of the smallest bikinis we had ever seen came walking down the beach and laid their beach towels down just a few feet in front of us and began to sunbathe. I remember Norm chuckling as he looked at me and said, "Wouldn't you figure this entire beach is available to these two, and they have to plop down right here in front of us... and our wives are sitting right over there."

We continued talking and a few minutes later one of the girls rolled over in a way that provided us a rather full view of some of her anatomy. One of the funniest moments of my life was how our conversation suddenly stopped, and both of us quickly averted our eyes down the beach to the left only to have a rather busty girl dressed in an even smaller swim suit, bounding towards us, chasing a beach ball. We then, simultaneously and without a word, burst out in laugher. Instantly we both knew how silly we must have looked and that clearly the forces of nature were going to make this a rather stressful day at the beach rather than a relaxing one. Of course to prevent this type of thing from ever happing to us again, we've since bought better pairs of sun glasses to protect us from these worldly temptations... or at least the wrath of our wives.

One of the most frustrating aspects of the Gospels for me is the silence that is so boldly present when it comes to how Jesus dealt with His sexuality. Most men will tell you that when it comes to temptation, it is sexuality that tends to be one of the greater weaknesses. All we know about Jesus from the Gospels is that He was single and presumably celibate. That's great and all, but what would be even more wonderful would be some info on how He did it!

For the most part, Jesus is normally presented as so pure and holy that He never dealt with the sexual thoughts that most of us face. The problem with this is that if He didn't deal with them then He had a major disconnect with one of the greatest temptations most men face. The struggle with sexual temptation is this: it's one of the few struggles that originate from within our bodies. In order for a man to develop an addiction to drugs or alcohol, he must first partake of those substances. After that has taken place, he can eventually develop an addiction where his body literally craves more of what it has experienced. The difference with sex is that a man can never have had sex in his life but the impulse is still there. It's as if he can become addicted to something even though he has never experienced it. Attraction is so basic, so sub-conscience, and so primal that lust can occur almost before a guy realizes what's going on.

The concept of how Jesus dealt with sex is compounded by the fact that in the Bible sex is painted in a very positive and encouraging light when it takes place in the proper circumstances, meaning that sex, attraction, lust, etc. are not necessarily bad things when they take place in the confines of marriage. Yet, Jesus was never married, which means it is very difficult to look to Him for an example of how to handle one of the biggest parts of the human experience, our sexuality.

That said, the Bible still contains some very interesting tales of interactions Jesus had with women that, although not sexual in nature, were none the less revolutionary. When we read the Bible, we need to remember the social setting then was much different than the Western culture we appreciate today in regard to women's rights. During Bible times, women were barely viewed as people. Instead, they were treated and perceived more like property than anything else, perhaps a half step above slaves and livestock. Let's not forget that when a man wanted to marry a woman, he would not court her, but purchase her from her father. The woman, of course, had no choice in this matter. In fact, one of the "rules" from the Old Testament stated that if a man raped an un-betrothed woman, his punishment was to pay the girl's father 50 shekels and marry her! (Deut 22: 28-29) How incredibly horrible did this have to be from the woman's perspective? She gets raped and after enduring that trauma, is forced to marry her rapist! So much for equality; this was on par with barbarianism. In general, women were not even allowed to talk to men outside of their family in public.

Imagine the social awkwardness that would have taken place when, in a world that was so harsh and cold toward women, along comes Jesus, a man who for the first time in their lives actually looks them in the eyes and smiles; a man, a holy man at that, who dares to violate the sacred laws and customs of the day, to crown them with dignity and show them compassion. We see Him consoling a widow who lost her only son, prior to raising him from the dead and giving him back to her. He allows a woman with a menstrual hemorrhage, which would have been ceremonially unclean in that era, to actually touch Him! In fact, she would have been considered so unclean that Jesus Himself would have been viewed as unclean for simply having contact with her! Then He shockingly takes the time to acknowledge her publicly in a crowd and bestow upon her the dignity of being a human being! All while making an important male figure wait. To most she would have been the ultimate outcast! But not to Jesus. To Jesus she was a broken human being who needed love and acceptance more than anything else.

He raises little girls from the dead, He saves prostitutes from certain death, He encourages women to stop waiting on Him and to sit and visit, He allows a woman of ill repute to publicly pour oil all over His head, He sits at a well and visits with not only a woman, but a woman who is from what is considered to be an inferior race, and not only is she of an inferior race, she is of questionable reputation making her an outcast even among her own people.

For some reason Jesus saw women differently than anyone in His culture ever had. He saw them as people, as love worthy, as broken, as deserving of dignity. In fact, when Jesus rises from the dead it is a woman who is the very first person He appears to!

The Bible makes it clear that Jesus had a very different perspective toward women than anyone else. But for me, two big questions remain: a) Where did He gain this unique perspective, and b) How did that affect His sexuality?

There is one passage I have discovered that I find quite interesting about Jesus and I think it might give a bit of insight as to where He developed the soft spot in His heart for women. "They answered and said to Him, 'Abraham is our father.' Jesus said to them, 'If you are Abraham's children, do the deeds of Abraham. But as it is, you are seeking to kill Me, a man who has told you the truth, which I heard from God; this Abraham did not do. You are doing the deeds of your father.' They said to Him, '**We were not born of fornication; we have one Father: God.**'" (John 8:39-41, bold emphasis added)

Here in John, Chapter 8, Jesus is in a pretty heated debate with the religious leaders when they make this statement that they weren't born of "fornication" which in Biblical times meant sex outside of marriage. The context of the passage is that they are debating with Jesus who is actually doing the will of the Father (God). So when they say that they were "not" born of fornication, the implication is that Jesus "was." Now keep in mind, Jesus was not Joseph's child and that the pregnancy of Mary, the mother of Jesus took place prior to their marriage. The Nativity story suggests that Mary's pregnancy was hidden and publicly covered up by the marriage, but I don't think it would have been a stretch that the story may have gotten out. And let's face it, in those days a girl claiming her pregnancy took place supernaturally while she was still a virgin probably would have been met with at least the same amount of skepticism as it would be today.

If that was the case, then Mary would have bore the immense pressure of having been branded a "loose" woman in an era where that sort of thing was incredibly devastating and could even be punishable by death. It was a huge burden for any woman who had given birth to a child out of wedlock, let alone a young lady who was probably between 13 and 16 as Mary likely would have been. With this reputation, both Mary and Jesus would have been the subjects of countless hours of gossip and scorn. Little Jesus growing up would have watched the horrific treatment His mother received as she walked through the market, went to the well, or did anything in public. He would have been both the witness and the recipient of the sneers and insults, the abusive language, the teasing and mocking of His peers, perhaps even physical abuse of being shoved, tripped, and punched. This treatment would have most likely multiplied exponentially after Joseph died and she no longer had the shelter of a husband to shield her.

The Bible indicates that Jesus also had brothers and sisters. (Matthew 13:55, 56) What we don't know is if these children would have been Joseph's from a previous marriage, making Jesus the youngest, or if they were children that Joseph and Mary had after they were married, making Jesus the oldest. What we do know is that these children would have most likely been conceived appropriately within the confines of marriage, making Jesus the only illegitimate child. As a result, Jesus would have even been subject to the scorn of even His own siblings as they tried to separate themselves from Him. As a bastard child,

Jesus Himself would have had one of the closest experiences possible for a man to relate to a woman of His day.

Imagine how His personal experiences, combined with what He likely witnessed His mother endure, might have sculpted His perspectives on the opposite gender. He wouldn't have had to speculate how it *might* feel to be an outcast, instead He, although innocent, would have known *first hand*. For many of us men, the physical struggle we deal with in regard to women comes from an innate desire to experience the sexual fulfillment we feel a woman can provide. But how would our view of women differ if we viewed them as equal victims of the social scorn we encountered growing up? Might that change our perception of them? Might that cause us to look upon them differently? This is especially true in a society where almost all of them could easily be viewed as victims of social injustice. Just like Jesus, their only mistake was to be born "wrong."

Perhaps the celibacy of Jesus did not emerge so much out of some sort of supernatural and divine discipline that empowered Him to master His own impulses as much as it was drowned out by the overwhelming heartbreak He might have felt for the women He knew. Perhaps He saw the broken heart before the pretty face. My personal opinion is that Jesus was the most authentic person that ever lived. One of the things about authentic people is that they follow their hearts and they pursue what they genuinely want. I have a hard time seeing Jesus resisting a desire He wanted because that would have been inauthentic. Instead, I suspect He pursued His true desires, which in His case, always proved to be perfect. If that is the case, then His celibacy would not have been because He resisted what He really wanted; rather, because He pursued what He really wanted. He would have been celibate not because He was denying Himself, but because He was fulfilling Himself.

Many of us have had close friendships with the opposite gender that were very deep and intimate, yet nonsexual. Although these friendships are rare, most of us can think of at least one time where this has happened in our lives. There also exists the much more common dynamic where close friendships were ruined once sex was introduced into the equation. The fact is that sex has a tendency to tweak our emotions and limit our ability to see relationships clearly. Often times, if our non-marital relationships are going to remain uninhibited, free, rich, and clear, sex cannot be part of the dynamic. For once it is, complicating factors begin to emerge that forever change the chemistry of the friendship, resulting in that awkward "ex-lover" experience that will forever hang over the relationship like a cloud.

It would appear in the case of Jesus that He knew marriage was not going to be an option for Him based upon what He was here to accomplish. It is also apparent that Jesus was extremely sensitive to relationships and sought to maximize His relational experience with everyone with whom He dealt. He would have known that to marry would have subjected His wife to unimaginable grief as she tried to walk with Him along His fateful road. In addition to this, marriage is meant to be a relationship that actually makes both halves a little better as one than they are alone. I would have to imagine life would be amazingly frustrating for a woman trying to be married to Jesus in that she would constantly live her life on a level that was so far below His. She would have never seen the world the way He did. One of the reasons many people don't get married is not because they don't want to but that it can be so difficult to find someone "like them" with whom to share their lives.

Who knows, perhaps Jesus really did want to get married but was unable to find anyone on His level, someone that could see the world and life with the same clarity, the same innocence, the same love. Instead, perhaps He handled each relationship He had in a manner that would maximize the depth of intimacy that each person could handle, free from the tangles and nearsightedness that can occur when sex is present. Perhaps His refraining from sex was not because He couldn't handle it, but because no partner would have been able to handle it.

Jesus' love for people was complete and full, meaning that the next morning His love would have remained the same as it had the night before. But would anyone else have been able to do that? There is a sense of ownership that seems to creep in upon having sex where seeds of jealousy and insecurity are planted. Let's face it, once we have sex with someone, that relationship is forever changed, never to be the same again. For the relationship to maintain the same intimacy, it must now continue on for life. If the relationship ends after sex, it will never have the same purity as it did before the act; it will forever be altered and almost always for the worse. In my previous book, *What If God Is Like This?*

I wrote a chapter on true love. I suggested that for love to really be unconditional, one must possess the ability to love all people the same, thus removing all conditions from any and all relationships. If someone becomes sexually intimate with another person, it not only changes the dynamic of the relationship between those two people, but the dynamic of every other relationship in the lives of those two people. Now, a platform has been reached that nobody else has access to. In essence, a condition has now been established that allows one to be sexually intimate with one person, but not another. Upon that occurrence, unconditional love for all others would be lost because a new condition would now exist for only that one person.

Is that why Jesus chose to remain celibate? Maybe the most important aspect of interacting with others on this earth was His relationships with them. Suppose He was so focused that nothing inhibited His relationships; that He refused to engage in the one thing that would change His relationship with every other person on earth, that being, to have a sexually intimate partner. This factor would suddenly place one person above all others in His life by granting them a level of intimacy with Him that no others would have ever had a chance to experience. Perhaps He "...so loved the world..." with such fervor that just one person could have never been singled out as the recipient of His deep affection for all.

9

God's Plan

"How are you doin'?" I asked, the words flowing off my tongue as they had a million times before with this programmed question. As the young widow looked at me and began to explain that she was hanging in there as best she could, I immediately felt stupid and awkward. I realized I had recklessly thrown the question out there to a woman that I hardly knew in the midst of one of the most difficult situations of her life: the loss of her husband.

As she began to answer the question as best she could, I knew I had asked it the same way as I had of any stranger in the store. I had asked it just to be friendly. Fortunately, I was able to recover as I really did feel compassion for her.

I was lucky to learn this lesson without causing this dear woman even more pain. I don't know if she caught my awkwardness and kindly let me off the hook, or if she was so distracted by her situation that she didn't even notice. Since then, I've tried to be much more careful about selecting my words in sensitive circumstances.

I wonder, how did Jesus handle situations like that? It seems that one of the most awkward positions for people is to be in the presence of someone who is truly suffering. We seem to have a real problem with it. I'm not sure if it is just that we don't want to have to face the fact that people do get cancer, or get sick, or die, or if it's that we feel guilty in light of true suffering. How big of a deal do we make about the trivial aspects of life? And how big of a deal do we not make about the things that matter most?

I can imagine Jesus a few days after the death of His earthly father, Joseph, and wonder if people threw out the cliché statements:

"I know this seems difficult, Jesus, but God works in mysterious ways."

"Just remember, Jesus, God won't give you more than you can handle."

"God has a plan for this, Jesus; it's all part of His will."

"Don't worry, Jesus. God works all things together for good."

I wonder if Jesus just smiled politely at their feeble attempts to comfort Him and accepted them as kind gestures, or if He, like so many of us, would have hid His boiling blood and confusion with the situation. I don't know many people who have experienced the loss of a loved one or have discovered they were stricken with some debilitating disease who were excited to hear that God is somehow behind this "blessing" in disguise. Was Jesus ever left as confused as the rest of us? Did He ever lock eyes with His comforter and strongly proclaim, "No! No, this was not the will of God, this was not His plan, and He is not behind this tragedy!" I wonder if He ever tore open a scroll and pounded His finger down on that first chapter of Genesis and announced that death, suffering, sickness, and the like were never part of God's plan, never!

Yet, somehow, probably out a sheer need to cope, religion has determined that suffering, pain, and death are parts of God's orchestration for us, events He has set in motion. Even in the middle of tragedy, we want to believe

He is still in control of everything, that within this gigantic universe we really aren't alone, that there really is Someone looking out for us. Some of the greatest frustrations of my life have been to watch the suffering of others. I've watched friends wither away at the hands of cancer and depart this world as broken shells of the people they used to be. I've watched parents helplessly stand by as a child was slowly taken from them at the hands of the same disease. I've prayed for countless people with all kinds of ailments with results that have been completely random. Sometimes it seems that situations improve and people recover and other times they don't. I think I'm bothered more by the lack of consistency in the healing than the fact there was ever an ailment to begin with.

I have to believe that for Jesus to fully have been able to appreciate and relate to the human experience there had to have been times where people were not healed. I wonder, when did He perform His first healing? Not only that, I wonder, when did He first realize His power would not only extend to the broken and hurt, but could also reach beyond the grave and retrieve those who had passed on? As a child and young man I wondered, did He just start healing people all of a sudden or did He have to work up to it? I would think that if He was performing miracles the whole time then surely there would be more stories of other amazing feats that took place in those lost years between twelve and thirty. Perhaps even Jesus was able to relate to the frustration of praying for someone only to see the suffering conclude in death. Who knows? Honestly, I hate to admit it, but there is a big part of me that wants to believe He had to practice this. For some reason, that just seems more human to me. Just like us, that with every task we encounter we have to practice and work at it to become proficient. There is a part of me that wonders/hopes that miracle working would be the same way.

But what we do know is that at some point, either because He decided to begin, or because He got the hang of it, Jesus began to successfully cure the ailments of those around Him, even raising the very dead. I wonder if that is one of the reasons He had a tendency to be so patient. Have you ever noticed when we read the Gospels, we never see Jesus in a rush to get anywhere? People would come clamoring up to Him and plead with Him to come and heal their loved ones, only to see Jesus kindly agree and begin sauntering in their direction. I can only imagine the frustration of Jarius, the Ruler as he came to ask Jesus to heal his ailing daughter only to have the Messiah become sidetracked by that woman in the crowd who crawled up and touched Him. Interestingly, the daughter of this extremely important ruler was twelve years old, while the ailment tormenting this nobody of a woman had also lasted twelve years, possibly showing Jesus' willingness to care for all, no matter their status. In my mind's eye, I can see Jarius fidgeting and pacing impatiently as he waits for Jesus to conclude His wonderful little conversation with this lady, who, by the way, probably could have waited another hour or so if she had been suffering for twelve years, while his little girl was clinging to life. I can imagine the look on his face as his servants approached and advised him that his daughter had indeed died. I wonder what he felt in that moment? Did his heart sink in complete brokenness? Did he suddenly look at this lowly hag with disdain and bitterness for costing his little girl her life? Perhaps he was mad at Jesus? After all, how could Jesus have not been more aware of the urgency of the matter? Why didn't he just tell the woman to wait where she was and that He would follow up with her later? After all, it appears the woman was healed the instant she touched Him. All He had to do was keep walking, and He could have healed two people. But no. No, He had to stop and talk, as if the whole world was supposed to run on His schedule. It's hard to say what all Jarius must have felt in that moment, but I can only imagine the dread mixed with hope he must have endured when Jesus looked at him with those pure and genuine eyes and told him it wasn't over yet.

You see, since Jesus knew God would go so far as to raise the dead through Him, it erased any sort of end line. Jesus could take His time in everything He did because nothing was beyond the possibility of God. How much clearer would our priorities become if we realized there were no real deadlines or make or break situations in our lives? How many people did I fail to visit in the hospital or spend time with while they were hurting simply because I "was too busy?" Jesus never suffered from this dilemma because He didn't keep a schedule. He freed Himself of all unnecessary responsibilities so that He could only focus on what mattered, that being people. He was never too busy to stop and deal with the person in need, and if the person He was on His way to heal died, He knew He could reach beyond death and still provide the necessary healing.

Today, we still apply the same time restrictions to God. When our loved ones suffer, we still view death as the finish line. We still desperately pray that He will somehow save this person before they perish and depart from this world forever, and if He doesn't, we probably feel those same feelings that Jarius most likely felt that day He found out Jesus was too late. "Thanks for nothing, God! I needed this healing and you failed me!"

If things haven't changed and we still feel the same urgings and emotions Jarius felt, shouldn't we ask, "What if Jesus still has the power to reach beyond the grave and heal?" In His day, He would reach beyond the grave and provide healing to the dead, but perhaps today He reaches beyond the grave and provides healing to the living. Perhaps is it our loved ones who have passed on that take Him by the hand and point Him to us. Perhaps from the other side they are the ones who ask Him to perform the miracle of healing in our lives, to reach beyond the grave and use His great power to provide us the healing we need, the healing that grants us peace and solace in our situations as we deal with loss.

If you think about it, that might be the more dramatic healing because that might be the more dramatic pain. I don't claim to know much about how Jesus works in these situations and I'd be lying if I didn't admit that there are times I still get angry and frustrated. In fact, as I'm writing this several friends are experiencing deep pain and suffering in their lives, and it's confusing. In my heart I'd like to believe that there was at least one point in the life of Christ where He experienced this feeling of helplessness but perhaps the answer now is not to know; instead to simply be still.

10

Jesus, the Recluse

If you haven't figured it out yet, one of my favorite things to do is to go backpacking. There is just nothing that can match the solitude, peace, and tranquility that comes with being fully plunged into the middle of nature. It is interesting how the pattern seems to work for me. As I get in the car and begin to drive out to some remote region, I find myself beginning to experience the first bits of relinquishing of the stress that is my constant companion. After several hours of driving I finally reach the destination at the end of some seldom traveled dirt road and exit the vehicle with a long stretch and a huge gulp of fresh air. Yet, this is not enough: I am still too close to society, to cars, stereo systems, and cell phone signals. I must retreat farther. So, with a grunt I sling the large backpack onto my shoulders, grab my ancient looking walking stick, and go down a fern lined forest trail into the wilderness. With each step, I feel more and more free. Out here there are no bills to pay, there are no meetings to keep, no phone calls to make. Out here my only responsibility is just not to get myself killed, which, by the way, doesn't require that much effort. Out here the birds serenade me, the wind whispers to me though the pine needles; out here creeks babble and call me to join them in their playful dance through boulders and stones while at night lulling me to sleep in my tent. The mountains and cliffs perform for me, using sunsets and moonrises to display their stunning grander. At night the heavens put the universe on display as countless stars, planets, and galaxies pop against the black canvass of space, silently displaying its awesome beauty to the chorus of a million cricket choir.

It is here that I find solitude; it is here that I am able to quiet my mind and focus on what truly matters in life. One of my favorite experiences is finding the high places, leaving camp and climbing a mountain that rises above all else.

From vantage points like these I love to sit quietly and gaze out at the beauty of creation. From here one can seen valleys, mountains, and canyons. Vultures that normally soar high overhead, are now specks hundreds of feet below. I can sit in these places for hours taking it all in.

One experience I had like this was in Israel of all places. In college, I had the wonderful opportunity to go to the Holy Land and part of our trip included the Sea of Galilee. I was a member of the cross country team for my small college, so each morning I would try to find time to run a few miles. One morning, I set out along a road that meandered along the edge of the water when a certain hill caught my eye. I noticed that near the top of this hill was a bit of a natural perch, the perfect place to sit and overlook the sea. I was certain it was the kind of place Jesus Himself would have retreated to early in the mornings to think and pray. So, off the road I went, climbing up the rocky hill through stalks of wispy yellow grass. Then, just a few hundred feet from my goal, I came across a barbed wire fence with a sign posted in a language I could not read. The sign, based on its general design, looked very much like a no trespassing sign back in the United States, but since I couldn't read it, I figured it probably said, "Welcome." Although this was Israel, so I suppose it could have also said, "Danger, Land Mines Present." Either way, through the fence I went. Looking back, I'm sure there was nothing suspicious about a foreigner scampering up a hill past an obvious barrier in a country on constant alert due to being surrounded by enemies. But that's neither here nor there.

When I finally arrived at my spot, I spend about 20 minutes sitting and overlooking the Sea of Galilee. In my mind, I imagined how similar things probably looked to Jesus in His day as so little had been developed here. I couldn't get past the very real possibility that He might have sat in this exact spot and looked out over the same waters I was looking at, the same shore line, the same cliffs in the distance, under the same sky. Honestly, it was one of the most spiritual moments of my entire life.

What is it about the rat race that seems to blind us to the obvious? Sadly, as much clarity as I am able to discover in these places, it seems so quickly lost when I return to society. I wonder if that happened for Jesus as well?

The Bible makes it pretty clear that He had a habit of getting away for some seclusion now and then. One of which was a 40-day jaunt into the wilderness by Himself! Now that's what I call getting away from it all. There is just something different about being completely alone for an extended period of time. Most of us never experience it anymore, especially in a world that allows us to wake up to music playing, get dressed to the TV, drive to and from work listening to the radio, and fall asleep watching the TV again. It's no wonder we have such hard times finding ourselves because we never actually spend time with ourselves. There is always a distraction, always something to occupy the mind. Is that how Jesus felt with people constantly trying to gain His attention? Was He ever overwhelmed by the crowds following Him everywhere He went? Is that why He liked to sneak away?

As I write this, I'm sitting alone on the deck of a cabin at the Junipine Lodge in Sedona, Arizona. Below me I can hear the rushing waters of Oak Creek and in front of me a lush green canyon framed by red cliffs fills in the back drop. It rained last night and the fragrance is still strong in the air. I'm here for a wedding and today I must return back to my everyday life. But I'm discovering that the key to living life is to ensure that there is no such thing as an "everyday" life.

The biggest lesson I've learned from my alone times is how to appreciate the miracles that are constantly around me, the ones I overlooked for so much of my life: the miracle of the bird that just picked up that twig to fashion it into a nest, the glory of each and every sunrise and sunset, the uniqueness of every giggle from a child, the beauty that is ever present all around us.

In the beginning when God created this place He declared that it was "good" and He was right. It most certainly is. Maybe that was why Jesus liked to get away now and then. Maybe He liked to find the high places once in awhile, the places with the views so that He could take a few moments to climb above the painting and admire the creation He of which He was now a part. And, like us, perhaps when He did this even He discovered a little more about Himself.

11

The Rock Star

Working in law enforcement you occasionally have the opportunity to come across some famous people. Sometimes it is pretty obvious, like if you are working at a big event or a concert of some sort. Sometimes you come across them in public as anyone else would and you recognize them by the entourage of people surrounding them. Other times it can be much more subtle, like if you are called to the home of one for something. This is where it can be rather interesting. There have been several times I have been called to an address and it wasn't until the person who answered the door told me their name that I realized I was talking to someone famous. Prior to this information,

I thought I was dealing with another average, ordinary person.

It's interesting, how once you realize who you are dealing with, there can be a slight temptation to begin to treat them differently than you would have had you remained ignorant of their status. What is also interesting is how normal even celebrities typically are in their own home setting. Over the years, I've discovered that we as the general public are the ones that tend to drive the celebrity ego more than anything. What must it be like to have millions of people want to know you not because they really care all that much about you, they just want to be part of the group?

It only took me a couple of encounters like these before I began to understand that people are just people and the world is really not all that much different than high school. Some people are more popular than others, but we are actually not all that different. We all live, we all die, and we all want to be accepted. Now when I come across the celebrity type, I'm not quite as enamored as I was when I was younger. I've gotten better at seeing famous people as regular people who just happen to be recognized more often than the average sort.

It appears that Jesus seemed to have a pretty good handle on how to deal with the celebrities of His day. Obviously, Jesus ended up becoming fairly well known Himself toward the end of His ministry, but even with that, He never seemed to be overly affected by dealing with people of influence. He seemed to have this innate ability to treat all people the same, the princes or the paupers. When dealing with the powerful religious leaders, He didn't hesitate to tell them what He thought. When He was under arrest and being hauled off from trial to trial, He wasn't intimidated by Herod as He was paraded into his court. When He had to face the powerful Pontius Pilate He refused to cower in the presence of the man who had the ability to save His life. Even when Pilate made this point quite clear to Jesus, His only response was that Pilate would have no power over Him if it wasn't granted from above. How is it that the lowly stepson of a carpenter from an obscure region of Israel could develop such moxie as to be un-phased by the power players of His day? Perhaps He simply didn't realize how powerful these men were? Though I'm quite certain that wasn't the case, another reason might be that He had an ability to see something in these people that most people didn't.

Perhaps Jesus was on to something when He pointed out to Pilate that his power came from elsewhere. Isn't that really the case with all people? Is anyone really famous or powerful in their own right? Honestly, what is it that makes someone powerful or famous? Isn't it just other people? Can anyone really be famous without the aid of others? Famous people aren't famous simply because they are; famous people are famous because we make them famous. We grant them our attention, our adoration, our praise. Without us, famous people are just people. How powerful would Pilate have been if nobody obeyed him? What if nobody listened to the powerful dictator? How powerful would he be then? Probably not much more than you or me. In the end, we are all still people. We are all created equal, all created in God's image.

The great irony of our Western Culture is that we preach and teach that all people are equal, that all people are the same. But there is hypocrisy in our spouting of these values in that we don't really practice them. If everybody is equal, then why do we clamor for the autographs of our favorite celebrities but ignore our garbage man? Interestingly, if my favorite celebrity and my garbage man were to both go on strike the same day I bet I can take a good guess as to who I would miss first! We, the masses, are the ones who ultimately decide who holds power and influence in our lives by how we react to and treat people. What are we willing to give to other people? Do we give them our money, our attention, our dignity? When people hold power over us it is normally because we grant them that power. We go ahead and agree that they have power over us and act accordingly. In some cases, such as the dictator, we do this out of the fear of what might be done to us if we didn't agree.

In the case of Jesus, there were people who were willing to obey the decree of Pilate to either kill Him or save His life. And when Pilate tried to hold this over His head, Jesus would have nothing of it. He quickly set the record straight on the fact that Pilate's power was not his own but came from elsewhere. I wonder if part of Jesus' ability to do this came from a complete lack of the fear of death? Sure, Pilate could make the call to have Jesus killed or saved, but that didn't make him any better of a person than anyone else. He just happened to have people that would do what he said.

That's one of the problems with fame and power. Once its holder becomes enlightened to the fact that they really don't possess these attributes, they become a slave to the people. They have to constantly give the people what they want, and if the tastes of the people change, it is up to the celebrity to conform to this new flavor. Should they fail, they quickly become yesterday's news and are thrust into the "has been" category, at best just a half step above the regular Joe, and at worst a laughing stock and an object of ridicule. For the man of power to remain a man of power, he must constantly keep the people that grant him that power under his thumb either by force or by favor. Fame and power are precarious positions for those who crave them because those who hold them can be forever afraid of the idea of losing them.

Jesus was free from this. He was free from the pressures of losing His fame. As a result, He conformed to nobody, not even the crowds. He simply lived His life as exactly who He was, fame or no fame, it made no difference. He was not here to win over the masses. He was here save them.

I think Jesus realized that what made Him special were not other people, but His "Father in Heaven." I suspect Jesus might have pointed out that when one person idolizes another they are not really lifting up the other person but lowering themselves. As two creatures created equally in God's image, if one exalts the other, doesn't that diminish God's image in the worshiper? But, how much different is it when we draw our value from the One who actually determines it, from the very God who created us? In that case, when we draw our value from something greater than we are, we no longer lower ourselves; but, rising up, we embrace who and what we really are and were meant to be.

12

The Unanswered Prayer

What must it feel like to have all of your prayers answered just the way you pray them? I've wondered about this a number of times, especially in times where I've prayed for a healing. I stood by helplessly a few years ago watching a co-worker of mine die of cancer. Week after week, month after month, she deteriorated in health as the disease mercilessly marched on. I had several visits with her at her home as she was ailing and on a couple of instances, at her request, wrapped her up in a hug and prayed that God would somehow remove the cancer. They were some of the hardest prayers of my life because in the back of my mind I feared they would not be answered. The Bible indicates that for prayer to work it must be accompanied by faith. Many people might cite the following verse and point out that my prayer and my co-worker were doomed from the start, due to my lack of faith: "But if any of you lacks wisdom, let him ask of God, who gives to all generously and without reproach, and it will be given to him. But he must ask in faith without any doubting, for the one who doubts is like the surf of the sea, driven and tossed by the wind. For that man ought not to expect that he will receive anything from the Lord, being a double-minded man, unstable in all his ways." (James 1:5-8)

Now, keeping that passage in context, it is about praying for wisdom, not healing; but, if faith is required for wisdom, it must certainly be required for healing. Perhaps my doubt cost my friend her life? The thought of that still bothers me sometimes, but in all honesty, I certainly hope God doesn't work quite like that. It would be rather unfair for my friend to have paid the ultimate price as a result of my skeptical prayers. I've never doubted that God lacked the power or ability to perform these miracles; most of my apprehension came in wondering if He would do it in this instance. I can't tell you how many times I wished I'd had the ability to confidently walk into her little house, pat her two dogs on the head, hand her the cup of egg drop soup she had requested before placing my hand on her head and commanding her back to full health. Jesus did that kind of thing all the time and it always worked.

What kind of assurance would come with the guarantee that your prayer would be answered no matter what? Jesus was so good at it that people would desperately come from miles around to see Him. Having Jesus pray for you didn't appear to be a last second gamble; it was a sure thing and everybody knew it! No matter what the issue, it seemed like Jesus always had the trump card of prayer.

"What? Our boat is about to sink? Stand by, allow Me to calm this storm."

"What do you mean we don't have enough food for everyone to eat? Let's just pray over these fish and loaves and PRESTO! Fine dining for all!"

"Did you say your servant was dying? Just a second, allow Me to just say the word from here."

"What's that? Lazarus died four days ago? Voila! He's back!"

Nobody I've ever known has had this kind of success when it comes to answered prayer. And, in fact, nobody I've ever known or heard of in our modern day has even come close to this kind of thing with the frequency or consistency Jesus did. When I ponder this, I come to two realizations:

1. Jesus was so far above me that I will never be able to relate to His success.
2. I am so far below Jesus that He will never be able to relate to my failure.

This sounds bad, but there is a part of me that wishes the Bible contained a few stories of how Jesus would handle unanswered prayers. That's actually the area with which I am much more familiar. All of us who have ever prayed have experienced a number of times, probably more often than not, that our prayers were not answered or at least not answered in the way we wanted. Wouldn't it be nice to be able to look to the Greatest Icon of all time to learn how to deal with these instances? Unfortunately, we can't, because all we ever see from Jesus is success when it comes to His prayer life... that is, with one exception. If you were to scour all the stories of Jesus you would only find one occasion where a prayer of His was not answered, and it was probably the most desperate prayer He ever uttered. "Then Jesus came with them to a place called Gethsemane, and said to His disciples, 'Sit here while I go over there and pray.' And He took with Him Peter and the two sons of Zebedee, and began to be grieved and distressed. Then He said to them, 'My soul is deeply grieved, to the point of death; remain here and keep watch with Me.' And He went a little beyond them, and fell on His face and prayed, saying, 'My Father, if it is possible, let this cup pass from Me; yet not as I will, but as You will.'" (Matthew 26:36-39)

How hugely ironic is it that the only prayer in the entire Bible that was not answered for Jesus was one He prayed for Himself? And it wasn't just any prayer; it was a prayer begging God to save His life. How did that feel for Jesus? Was it strange for Him to have a prayer met with silence after having so many others answered? How incredibly alone must He have felt in the moment of His greatest need, to turn to His Father in heaven and be met with nothing? Perhaps Jesus can relate to me more than I imagined... perhaps He knows exactly the type of emptiness and abandonment that can accompany heaven's silence. Perhaps He truly does understand what it's like to cry out for help in darkness only for your words to evaporate into the emptiness.

Yes, it would appear that Jesus may have experienced this feeling more rarely than the rest of us, but at the time He did experience it He had as much riding on it as anyone could. As much as I hate that He went through this, I am comforted that He can relate to my experiences. But relating is one thing; the big question is how did He handle it?

When Jesus enters the Garden of Gethsemane He appears to be the least composed He's ever been. The disciples are acutely aware that something is wrong with their friend; He is acting in ways He never has before. Let's go back to our previous scripture: "Then Jesus came with them to a place called Gethsemane, and said to His disciples, 'Sit here while I go over there and pray.' And He took with Him Peter and the two sons of Zebedee, and began to be grieved and distressed. Then He said to them, 'My soul is deeply grieved, to the point of death; remain here and keep watch with Me.'" (Matthew 26:36-38)

The Book of Luke even documents that Jesus began to sweat drops of blood during this event. Now as Jesus appears to be at His weakest point in life, the disciples are to the contrary. They have never been more bold and confident than they are right now. Just a few minutes before going to the Garden they all vowed that they would follow Jesus to the death! These guys are committed! They are feelin' good! They are confident! Can't you just hear it in their voices? "We will die for you!" They are so confident in fact that when Jesus begs them to pray with Him, they use it as an opportunity to drift off to la-la land and catch a few zzz's. And who can blame them? They had just finished a long day that concluded with a Passover feast where several cups of wine were ceremonially consumed. These guys are battling a food coma. So here they sit and we get to observe one man at His weakest point in life uttering up prayers to heaven that are not being answered while another group of men at the strongest point in their lives are taking a nap instead of praying.

After an hour or so of this, something remarkable happens: "Then He came to the disciples and said to them, 'Are you still sleeping and resting? Behold, the hour is at hand and the Son of Man is being betrayed into the hands of sinners. Get up, let us be going; behold, the one who betrays Me is at hand!' While He was still speaking, behold, Judas, one of the twelve, came up accompanied by a large crowd with swords and clubs, who came from the chief priests and elders of the people." (Matthew 26:45-47)

Where did this guy come from?! I thought this was the guy who was just sweating blood and groveling to God, pleading to be bailed out of His situation. Now look at Him! He's bold, He's strong, and instead of running from the problem He actually rises up, gathers His men, and goes out to meet the threat. The disciples, who had just an hour before been as strong as they ever had been, ready to die if necessary, are now trembling with fear. In a moment they will all flee, leaving Jesus alone to confront His accusers.

What had happened here? How could a man that was so weak suddenly become so strong and how could men that were so strong suddenly become so weak? What was the difference? They'd eaten the same meal, they'd gone to the same garden, they believed the same things, yet one prayed and the others didn't.

What is strange, though, is that the prayer was not even answered! God did not deliver Jesus from His fate as He had requested. Yet, somehow Jesus grew stronger during the encounter.

You see, for most of us when we pray, the purpose of the prayer is to change our circumstances. From Jesus to you or me, we all have our cups that we pray for God to take away. For Jesus it was the cross, for some it is the loss of a loved one, or cancer, or financial issues; whatever the case, we have all issued prayers for God to take away the dilemma we are too weak to handle. We have all felt the angry frustration that comes when nothing happens. But in Jesus we see the perfect example of dealing with unanswered prayer. In Jesus we see that when God failed to transform the circumstances, He instead transformed Jesus. Instead of making the problem go away or get smaller, He made Jesus stronger. Through the pain of desperate and unanswered prayer, Jesus was transformed from a man sweating blood to a man boldly confronting His problem.

So, the next time you find yourself in that dark place, that place where God seems too distant and far away to hear your prayer and change your circumstances, it may be just the opposite. He may be so close that He's changing you.

13

The Faith to Believe

"For God so loved the world, that He gave His only begotten Son, that whoever believes in Him shall not perish, but have eternal life." (John 3:16)

What does it mean to "believe" in Jesus? You hear it said all the time, "In order to be saved, you just gotta *believe* in Jesus. You can't doubt, you just gotta *believe*." But what does that really mean? I have a fear that the word *believe* in Christianity has come to actually mean "convince yourself" in the same way one might try to convince him or herself that there is a Tooth Fairy, or Santa, or in the same way that someone might try to convince themselves they aren't sick, or they are not getting old, or they don't have an addiction. I'm afraid that when it comes to religion, the word *believe* has come to mean that we must force ourselves to accept something in spite of what evidence or even our conscience might tell us is otherwise impossible. As a result, I fear this has led many to flee anything that might create or introduce doubt into our minds. We guard against exposing ourselves to other schools of thought out of the fear of being led astray. But truth is truth. Shouldn't it be that when one examines other considerations, the truth can shine even brighter?

For much of my life, my "belief" in Christianity was more out of a fear not to believe. I was afraid that if I didn't believe enough there would literally be hell to pay. This created a tendency to shy away from trying to think for myself and question anything that fell outside the safe boundaries of my Christian world. What I've since come to realize is that this position actually stunted my personal growth and ultimately my relationship with Christ. It hurt much more than it helped.

We live in a world where, unfortunately, there are a number of very bitter, angry, negative, and vengeful people who not only "believe" in Jesus, they believe He was the Son of God. Heck, most atheists actually believe in Jesus if it means the guy actually existed, but that's where their faith ends. Sadly, at least in the America, there is not often a big difference between the Christian culture and the secular culture. But why is this? Why is there often so little, if any, difference between church goers and non-church goers, especially in the ways they treat one another, the ways they conduct themselves at work, in their marriages, and other social settings? Why? One reason might be that the *only* difference between some Christians and everyone else is that they believe that Jesus was the Son of God. That's it! That's the only difference. It's just like believing in aliens wouldn't have a profound effect on the type of human being someone is. Yes, that belief might have an effect on a few aspects and habits in someone's life, but would it really have a profound effect on the core character of who they are? Not likely. What if there is more to the word *believe* when it comes to having a faith in Christ? What if it is something much deeper than its common understanding promotes?

One of the things that I find immensely profound about the life Jesus lived was that one would not have to believe

He was the Son of God in order to benefit from His teachings. Jesus taught love. "Love God, love your neighbor, and love your enemy." His teachings can pretty much be summed up as "love everybody." You don't have to have "faith" in a religion in order to love people. Instead, what it really takes is guts. It takes courage to step out and extend love to those with whom we struggle to get along. It's even harder when it's someone who wishes harm or ill will toward us.

Again the question I must ask is, "Why?" Why is it so hard for us to do this? What is the ultimate reason? I've thought a lot about this and the more I consider it the more I am led to the conclusion that the answer is: we are afraid. We are afraid to make ourselves vulnerable to those types of people. We are afraid that they will take advantage of us or hurt us. We are afraid that they will play dirty even when we try to play nice. Fear is the main obstacle that holds us back from loving like Jesus did. And it's for good reason. There are plenty of people in this world who will quickly and eagerly take the opportunity to inflict harm on those who will allow it.

But fear doesn't only hold us back in situations where there are people who wish us harm. Fear also rises up in any situation in which we feel the need for self preservation.

Let's consider this story from Mark, Chapter 1: "And a leper came to Jesus, beseeching Him and falling on his knees before Him, and saying, 'If You are willing, You can make me clean.' Moved with compassion, Jesus stretched out His hand and touched him, and said to him, 'I am willing; be cleansed.'" (Mark 1:40, 41)

Now, let's take a second and examine what just happened. Most of my life, I was so distracted by the miracle that I didn't fully see all that this encounter detailed. Here was a guy with leprosy. In a day and age where people would avoid him at all costs, Jesus actually reaches out and touches the guy! I immediately think of all the times I've been hesitant to even shake hands with someone I thought had dirty hands. Why? Simply put, because I was afraid. Afraid of getting sick, or catching cooties, or just being associated with certain people. It was fear that held me back. Jesus was never afraid to reach out to the unlovable. I mean, He actually held out His hand and touched a guy with leprosy! That tells me the love Jesus had for this guy was greater than any fear He might have had about catching the ailment. Now, some could easily say Jesus didn't have to worry about getting sick because He had the power to heal. I really hope that wasn't the case. If Jesus had some sort of magic plastic wrap that protected Him from the risk of contracting something, then to me it cheapens His grace. But if He was just as likely as you or me to get sick and die of some terrible condition, then it means His love for others was even greater than His love for His own life! Remember when Jesus spoke these words? "And He summoned the crowd with His disciples, and said to them, 'If anyone wishes to come after Me, he must deny himself, and take up his cross and follow Me. For whoever wishes to save his life will lose it, but whoever loses his life for My sake and the gospel's will save it.'" (Mark 8:34, 35) And remember this scripture, too: "He who has found his life will lose it, and he who has lost his life for My sake will find it." (Matthew 10:39)

To find life we must lose it! I think what Jesus might be telling us here is that if we are going to follow Him, and I mean truly follow Him, it will end up costing us our very lives. To love the way Jesus loved requires us to love others more than life itself. It means we will even reach out and touch those who have sickness that could claim our own health; it means that we will love enemies who may take the opportunities to harm us. The fact is, this is a cruel world and if we love like Jesus, it may very well take our lives from us. Thus, we take up our cross. We accept our fate and, like Jesus, we freely and willingly lay down our lives. And in exchange, we get the opportunity to truly, fully, and completely live a life to the full! Is it any wonder why He warned people to first consider "the cost" before following Him? (Luke 14:28) The fear of death is often what holds us back from this, but oddly, we are all going to die anyway, so what do we really have to lose?

Perhaps this is what Jesus meant when He invited us to take up our crosses and join Him on His humble path to change the world. Not just to "believe" something, but to sell out to it—to buy into a philosophy that has the power to change the world, the philosophy of love.

Is this what it means to "believe" in Jesus? Not just to accept that He really existed, or to convince ourselves of certain characteristics and attributes He might have had, but to recognize and understand the message of love that He taught? As beautiful as it sounds, love is not all rainbows and sunshine. Love is hard. As Jesus bravely and heroically demonstrated, love lived out completely may very well cost us our life. But it may grant it as well.

Extra-Ordinary

Taking up the task of writing about a man who is at least the greatest human being ever to live and at best the very Son of God has been a bit of a challenging one. In my heart, I believe Jesus to be God in the flesh, so I recognize any attempt to examine His humanity also runs the risk of diminishing His divinity, something I would never intentionally do.

I feel it is important that the reader knows my main purpose in attempting to examine Christ as a human being was not to lower Him as God, but instead to push myself farther as a human created in His image. I feel I owe it to God to do my best to become the most authentic human I can be based on who He created me to be and the example Jesus set. To do that, I felt it necessary to examine the greatest paragon of our species to learn how He handled this fleshly home in which we all indwell. I recognize to do so must be done with great care to preserve and maintain the honor He is due.

On the other hand, I also recognize that for many people in this world, Jesus is just another figure in history, one of several personalities who has worked His way into the eternal memory of man with His lasting mark on this world. And to others, He is a mythical character, wrought with magical powers to heal the sick and raise the dead. To them, He is merely another fable of human history. Others view Him in a very negative light. They see Him as the figurehead of a religion with a very seedy past, one that has condoned genocides, and promotes intolerance, condemning those who fail to accept its teachings to the very fires of hell.

Still there are more who view Christ as a great teacher who taught love and acceptance, but that He was nothing more than just a good man who lived long ago.

I willingly will concede that for the skeptics out there it might hard to take seriously a guy who is most famous for walking on water. Sadly, due to all the clutter that surrounds His life, many people dismiss Him as either just a teacher or a fanatic or maybe someone who never even existed at all. As a result, the baby is thrown out with the bath water and a true treasure is missed.

So for those out there who are still searching, still yearning, and still lacking peace in their lives, may I encourage you to take a second look at this remarkable man? If you can't believe He was God, if you can't believe in the miracles, if you can't believe He rose from the dead, that's okay. But what can you believe? Can you believe He existed? It's undeniable there are plenty of sources that provide ample evidence even beyond the Bible to support that truth including: Flavius, Josephus, Lucian, Cornelius Tacitus, and Plinius Secundus to name a few.

And what about His teachings? Can you believe those? After all, we can still see and read the words that are attributed to Him today.

Personally, I believe all one needs to discover how remarkable Jesus was, is to examine the stuff He said and the circumstances in which He said it. Don't worry about the miracles for now. Just look at the teachings. Jesus was raised in one of the more violent times in human history. He was raised in a world where people were fed to lions as entertainment. It was a bloodthirsty realm filled with bitterness, rage, and oppression. As a child He would have been read to from the Holy Scriptures about military campaigns commanded by God in which cities were completely wiped out, even the women and children slaughtered, where God would rain down His wrath on those who crossed Him. And in the midst of this barbaric and chaotic time one man was somehow able to develop a perspective that was so drastically different, a perspective of complete and unconditional love! And not only did He come up with this, He had the guts to share it and teach it publicly, knowing that it would cost him His very life. Then, even in the process of being tortured to death, He still found in His heart the ability to forgive. Simply amazing!

Yes, to the skeptics, I would dare you to take a chance and study Jesus as just a regular human being. But please, at least take the time to study Him. If anyone does, I'm confident they won't be able to remain there for long. I'm confident that the more one learns about this amazing man the less certain they will become that He was just simply a man. I'm convinced that in searching the humanity of

Christ, His divinity will be discovered, and by embracing this man, one will find God.

Acknowledgements

Special Thanks to:

Gary Thompson—Thanks for your continued assistance with the website, brother! You are a life saver. And you have the best rates in town!

Evelyn Nikkel—Thank you for letting me share your story my friend. It has been a wonderful experience getting to know you. God Bless you and your ministry to the wonderful people of Pella, Iowa!

Victoria Lee—Thank you for taking the time to endorse this thing, my friend. Your story and your ministry are so encouraging to so many.

Dave Curtiss — Thanks for the investments you've made into countless youth and youth pastors. You have been a fantastic mentor to so many. Mostly thanks for being so authentic. Having your endorsement is a true honor.

Heather Bixler — Thank you so much for your ministry to moms all over the country. You bless so many with your blogs and books. I am so blessed to have your endorsement and your friendship!

Marge Webb — Marge, thank you for the new friendship we've been able to develop over the past year. Thanks for sharing your keen eye to help clean up my error-filled manuscript!

Norm Rumsey — Thanks always for the wilderness excursions and the time spent visiting around a campfire. Also, thanks for your keen sense of where to sit at the beach.

Dan Antrim, Brian Hartman, and Father Mike — Thank you all for the countless lunch time conversations. I get so much out of our talks, and I enjoy the way you guys make me think about things.

Glen Aubrey and the Creative Team Publishing Staff — You guys did such a great job on Book Number 1 that I decided to sign up for round 2. Thanks for all your help in bringing these projects into fruition.

To all my friends and family — who supported, encouraged, and helped spread the news of "What If God Is Like This?" Without the help of all of you making Book 1 a success, Book 2 may have never come. I'm so blessed to have so many wonderful people in my life!

Lastly, to my wife and kids — Thank you for once again putting up with my long hours working on these projects. I love you all more than words. You four are my earthly inspiration!

The Author

Will Hathaway is a man who has worn many hats. Born the third of four children to a hardworking cattle rancher and his wife near the foothills of the Patagonia Mountains in southern Arizona, he quickly learned what it meant to work with the tools God gave you, your hands. He spent most of his childhood and young adult years driving fence posts and breaking horses.

It wasn't until Will left home to attend Grand Canyon University in Phoenix that he realized how unique his upbringing truly had been. While pursuing a degree in Marketing/Business, he met and then married the love of his life, Karra. It was through Karra that he obtained his first job in ministry, cleaning toilets at his church and serving as Youth Pastor to Junior and Senior High School students.

In 1999, Will felt led to pursue his lifelong passion of full-time ministry and headed off to attend Grace Theological Seminary in Warsaw, Indiana. Although he enjoyed his schooling, he took advantage of an offer to take a full-time position as a family life minister for a large church in Blytheville, Arkansas. Will and Karra remained in Arkansas for a year when they were surprised by the news of the upcoming birth of their first child.

They moved back to Arizona to be near family for the new baby. Will took a job in the investing/insurance market, but this vocation left him feeling empty and unfulfilled. During this time he continued his ministry pursuits as a volunteer youth pastor for their local church. The horrible events of 9/11/2001 became deciding factors that ended his short career as an investor.

Soon after, news started to spread that several local fire and police departments were hiring so, on a whim, he took a chance and was hired on as a police officer at a local department. Since his introduction to the police department in 2002, Will has served in many capacities including SWAT Negotiations.

Through the changes in his life, two things have remained consistent: 1) his call to ministry, with more than fourteen years in ministry beginning as a junior high and high school youth pastor and eventually as a college and career pastor; 2) his passion for his career in law enforcement.

Will is a family man with a strong sense of loyalty, especially when it comes to his wife, Karra, and their three children. He is an avid outdoorsman who enjoys spending time backpacking and camping in the New Mexico Wilderness. Many times he can be seen breaking horses on his parent's ranch, which still runs cattle today.

Will's diverse and multifaceted backgrounds provide him with unique perspectives on the world and God's interaction with it. Always seeking to gain a better understanding of his Creator, he is willing to ask the tough questions, many of which inspire his books.

Speaking Engagements and Products

Schedule Will Hathaway to speak at your event. Will Hathaway speaks for church services, conferences, Christian camps, and retreats.

Contact Will Hathaway at
www.Will-Hathaway.com.

Products:

- *What If God Is Like This?—Meet the God You've Never Known* is the first book in Will's series entitled, Released From Religion. It asks the tough questions many have wanted to ask as they contemplate who God really is.

- *The Human Side of Christ—Meet the Guy behind the God* is the second book of the series. This book peels back the divine cloak of mystery surrounding Christ and His existence as God in the flesh, and focuses on the human personality that walked the earth. It asks, "Who was this man?" "What was He like?" "How can we relate to Him?" Momentarily view Christ as a man rather than as God and relate to Him human-to-human in very special and basic ways. Discover that studying His humanity actually enhances the perspective of His divinity.

- *When Dead Men Walk—The Return to Authentic Humanity* is the third book in the series. This book builds off The Human Side of Christ and considers the fact that all people have lost touch with the true human spirit that God gave man when man was created. Man was made in the "image of God." Therefore, imperfections are not a result of being human; rather, humans are not human enough! This book takes the reader on a journey back to our true roots. It provides us a window back in time to view the very first people of God's creation. It also reveals our own souls so we can see the divine creature that lives within each of us.

CPSIA information can be obtained at www.ICGtesting.com
Printed in the USA
BVOW080501100613

322812BV00002B/5/P

9 780988 493421